VANCOUVER

2nd edition

Pierre Longnus
Paul-Éric Dumontier
François Rémillard

ULYSSES
TRAVEL PUBLICATIONS
Travel better... enjoy more

Editorial *Series Director:* Claude Morneau; *Project Supervisor:* Pascale Couture; *Editor:* Jennifer McMorran.

Research and Composition *Author:* Pierre Longnus, François Rémillard, Paul-Éric Dumontier

Production *Design:* Patrick Farei (Atoll Direction); *Proofreading:* Jennifer McMorran, Sarah Kresh, Tara Salman; *Translation:* Jennifer McMorran, Tracy Kendrick, Danielle Gauthier, Emmy Pahmer; *Update:* Sarah Kresh; *Cartography:* André Duchesne, Patrick Thivierge (Assistant); *Graphics:* Steve Rioux; *Layout:* Tara Salman.

Illustrations *Cover Photo:* Troy and Mary Parlee (Reflexion); *Chapter Headings:* Jennifer McMorran; *Drawings:* Lorette Pierson.

Thanks to SODEC and the Department of Canadian Heritage for their financial support.

Distributors

AUSTRALIA:
Little Hills Press
11/37-43 Alexander St.
Crows Nest NSW 2065
☎ (612) 437-6995
Fax: (612) 438-5762

BELGIUM AND
LUXEMBOURG:
Vander
Vrijwilligerlaan 321
B-1150 Brussel
☎ (02) 762 98 04
Fax: (02) 762 06 62

CANADA:
Ulysses Books & Maps
4176 Saint-Denis
Montréal, Québec
H2W 2M5
☎ (514) 843-9882,
ext.2232 or
1-800-748-9171
Fax: 514-843-9448
www.ulysse.ca

GERMANY AND AUSTRIA:
Brettschneider
Fernreisebedarf
Feldfirchner Strasse 2
D-85551 Heimstetten
München
☎ 89-99 02 03 30
Fax: 89-99 02 03 31

GREAT BRITAIN AND
IRELAND:
World Leisure Marketing
9 Downing Road
West Meadows, Derby
UK DE21 6HA
☎ 1 332 34 33 32
Fax: 1 332 34 04 64

ITALY:
Centro Cartografico del
Riccio
Via di Soffiano 164/A
50143 Firenze
☎ (055) 71 33 33
Fax: (055) 71 63 50

NETHERLANDS:
Nilsson & Lamm
Pampuslaan 212-214
1380 AD Weesp (NL)
☎ 0294-465044
Fax: 0294-415054

SCANDINAVIA:
Scanvik
Esplanaden 8B
1263 Copenhagen K
DK
☎ (45) 33.12.77.66
Fax: (45) 33.91.28.82

SPAIN:
Altaïr
Balmes 69
E-08007 Barcelona
☎ 454 29 66
Fax: 451 25 59

SWITZERLAND:
OLF
P.O. Box 1061
CH-1701 Fribourg
☎ (026) 467.51.11
Fax: (026) 467.54.66

U.S.A.:
The Globe Pequot Press
6 Business Park Road
P.O. Box 833
Old Saybrook, CT 06475
☎ 1-800-243-0495
Fax: 1-800-820-2329

Other countries, contact Ulysses Books & Maps (Montréal), Fax: (514) 843-9448

© February 1998, Ulysses Travel Publications
All rights reserved. Printed in Canada
ISBN 2-89464-120-6
Canadian Cataloguing in Press see p 6

PRINTED IN CANADA

"It has the combined excellence of Nature's gift and man's handiwork."

Stephen Leacock on Vancouver in
My Discovery of the West (1937)

TABLE OF CONTENTS

Help make Ulysses Travel Guides even better!

The information contained in this guide was correct at press time. However, mistakes can slip in, omissions are always possible, places can disappear, etc. The authors and publisher hereby disclaim any liability for loss or damage resulting from omissions or errors.

We value your comments, corrections and suggestions, as they allow us to keep each guide up to date. The best contributions will be rewarded with a free book from Ulysses Travel Publications. All you have to do is write us at the following address and indicate which title you would be interested in receiving (see the list at the end of guide).

Ulysses Travel Publications
4176 Rue Saint-Denis
Montréal, Québec
Canada H2W 2M5
www.ulysse.ca
e-mail: guiduly@ulysse.ca

Canadian Cataloguing in Publication Data

Longnus, Pierre
       Vancouver   2nd edition
       (Ulysses travel guides)
       Includes index
       Translation of: Vancouver
       Includes index.
       ISBN 2-89464-120-6
       1. Vancouver (B.C.) - Guidebooks. 2. Vancouver (B.C.)
       - Tours. I. Title. II. Series.
FC3847.18.D8513 1998   917.11'33044   C98-940216-9
F1089.5.V22D8513 1998

LIST OF MAPS

LEGEND

✪	Provincial or State Capital	✈	Airport
✪	National Capital	⛴	Ferry
▲	Mountain	◉	Skytrain
ℹ	Information	🛄	Train Station
⊘	Beach	🚌	Bus Station

TABLE OF SYMBOLS

🏝	Ulysses' favourite
☎	Telephone number
🐕	Pets allowed
⚏	Fax number
♿	Wheelchair accessible
≡	Air conditioning
⊙	Ceiling fan
≋	Pool
ℜ	Restaurant
⊛	Whirlpool
ℝ	Refrigerator
K	Kitchenette
:P	Parking
△	Sauna
☺	Exercise room
tv	Colour television
pb	Private bathroom
sb	Shared bathroom
ps	Private shower
½b	half-board (lodging + 2 meals)
bkfst	Breakfast

ATTRACTION CLASSIFICATION

★	Interesting
★★	Worth a visit
★★★	Not to be missed

HOTEL CLASSIFICATION

Unless otherwise indicated, the prices in this guide are for one room in the high season, double occupancy, not including taxes.

RESTAURANT CLASSIFICATION

$	$10 or less
$$	$10 to $20
$$$	$20 to $30
$$$$	$30 or more

Unless otherwise indicated, the prices in this guide are for a meal for one person, including taxes but excluding drinks and tip.

All prices in this guide are in Canadian dollars.

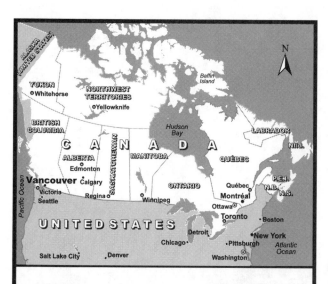

Where is Vancouver ?

British Columbia

Capital : Victoria
Languages : English and French
Population : 3,933,000 inhab.
Area : 950,000 km²
Currency : Canadian dollar

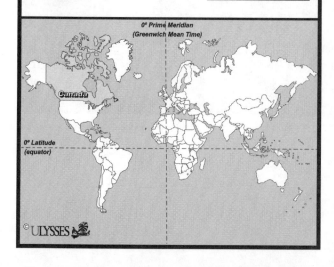

© ULYSSES

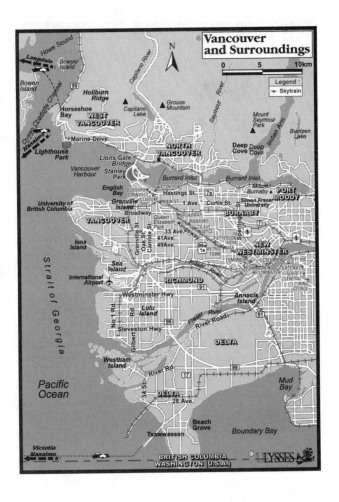

PORTRAIT

Vancouver is truly a new city, one framed by the mighty elements of sea and mountains. As part of one of the most isolated reaches on the planet for many years, the city has over the last 100 years, developed close ties with the nations of the largest ocean on Earth, and is fast becoming the multicultural metropolis of the Pacific Rim. Although its history is tied to the development of British Columbia's natural resources, most residents were lured here by the magnificent setting and the climate, which is remarkably mild in a country known for its bitter winters and stifling summers. Vancouver, where Asia meets America, is a city well worth discovering.

GEOGRAPHY

Canada's West coast, bounded by the 49th parallel to the south and the Alaskan border to the north, is dominated by the Coast Mountains, a chain of peaks west of the Rockies, which form an almost unbroken barrier between the Pacific and the hinterland. The vast delta of the Fraser River does break it and thus proves suitable for human habitation; Vancouver was founded in this favourable location. The city is now the third largest in Canada, with a population of nearly two million in the metropolitan area. It is also the only major city in the country whose eyes are decidedly turned toward the Pacific.

Pacific-minded though it is, Vancouver does not actually face right onto the ocean, but is separated from the sea by Vancouver Island, where Victoria, the capital of British Columbia, is located. Vancouver, the province's economic hub, lies on the Strait of Georgia, an arm of the sea separating Vancouver Island from the mainland. Its population is scattered across two peninsulas formed by Burrard Inlet to the north and False Creek to the south.

Point Grey, the larger, more southerly peninsula, is home to the University of British Columbia and sprawling residential neighbourhoods. On the smaller peninsula to the north, visitors will discover a striking contrast between the east end, with its cluster of downtown skyscrapers, and the west end, occupied by the lovely, unspoiled woodlands of Stanley Park. The situation of the city, surrounded by water and connected to the rest of the country by bridges and ferries, has led to a steady increase in the price of land in the centre and to major traffic problems for commuters from the city's suburbs and satellite towns. Finally, it is worth noting that Vancouver is only about 30 kilometres from the U.S. border (and less than 200 kilometres north of Seattle).

Vancouver boasts an exceptionally mild climate, with average temperatures of 3°C in January and 17°C in July. There is very little snow, though there is a lot of rain (annual average: 163 days of precipitation) and the summers are temperate and sunny. Clouds that form over the ocean are blown inland by westerly winds, when they hit the Coast Mountains they precipitate causing generally grey weather.

Plants thrive in this wet climate, and its wide variety of trees and flowers make Vancouver a vast, luxuriant garden where everything grows to be that much bigger than elsewhere. Not only are there species indigenous to the temperate rain forest (the northern counterpart of the equatorial forest) like enormous Douglas firs, red cedars, giant thuyas, and western hemlocks but over the decades, countless European and Asian plants have been imported to satisfy the local residents' passion for gardening. The numerous private and public ornamental gardens in and around Vancouver are thus adorned with North American, European and Asian species, to name but a few.

HISTORY AND ECONOMIC DEVELOPMENT

Indigenous Peoples

Over 10,000 years ago, a number of tribes, whose history all but disappeared along with the ice that once covered a large part of the northern hemisphere, travelled across the Bering Strait from Asia and scattered across North America, forming the numerous native nations and pre-Columbian civilizations of this continent. There is some doubt, however, as to whether or not native civilization on the West Coast originated with these vast waves of immigration. According to one theory, the ancestors of the West Coast tribes came here more recently (around 3000 B.C.) from islands in the Pacific. Proponents of this hypothesis base their argument on the natives' art, traditions and spoken languages, which are not unlike those of the indigenous peoples of the Pacific islands.

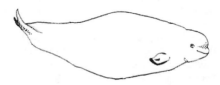

Beluga

When the first Europeans arrived here in the late 18th century, the region that would become Vancouver was inhabited by the Salish (the other native language families on the Pacific coast are Haida, Tsimshian, Tlingit, Nootka-Kwakiutl and Bellacoola). Like their compatriots, the Salish favoured this region for its remarkably mild climate and abundance of belugas, salmon, seals, fruit and other resources. This beneficial environment, combined with the barrier formed by the nearby mountains, enabled the coastal tribes to thrive. Not only was their population quite large, but it was also significantly denser than that of other native nations in central and eastern Canada.

In 1820, there were some 25,000 Salish living on the shores of the Fraser River, from its mouth south of Vancouver all the way up into the Rockies. Like other native tribes, the Salish were sedentary and lived in villages of red cedar longhouses. They traded with other natives along the coast during potlatches, festive ceremonies lasting weeks on end and marked by the exchange of gifts.

Belated Exploration

The 18th century saw an increase in exploration and colonization all over the world as European sea powers hungering for natural riches and new territories scoured the planet. The African shores were well charted, and no stone had been left unturned on the east coast of North America. There was, however, an immense area that still seemed inaccessible: the far-off and mysterious Pacific Ocean. Some of the many peoples inhabiting its shores were completely unknown to French, Spanish and English navigators. The Panama Canal had not yet been dug, and sailing ships had to cover incredible distances, their crews braving starvation, just to reach the largest of the Earth's oceans.

The voyages of French navigator Louis Antoine de Bougainville and English explorer James Cook, removed some of the mystery surrounding these distant lands. After Australia (1770) and New Zealand (1771), Cook explored the coast of British Columbia (1778). He did not, however, venture as far as the Strait of Georgia, where Vancouver now lies.

In 1792, Cook's compatriot George Vancouver (1757-1798) became the first European to trod upon the soil that would give rise to the future city. He was on a mission to take possession of the territory for the King of England, and by so doing put an end to any plans the Russians and Spaniards had of laying claim to the region. The former would have liked to extend their empire southward from Alaska, while the latter, firmly entrenched in California, were looking northward. Spanish explorers had even made a brief trip into Burrard Inlet in the 16th century. This far-flung region was not coveted enough to cause any bloody wars, however, and was left undeveloped for years to come.

The Vancouver region was hard to reach not only by sea, but also by land, with the virtually insurmountable obstacle of the Rocky Mountains blocking the way. Imagine setting out across the immense North American continent from Montreal, following the lakes and rivers of the Canadian Shield, and exhausting yourself crossing the endless Prairies, only to end up barred from the Pacific by a wall of rock several thousand metres high. In 1908, the fabulously wealthy fur merchant and adventurer Simon Fraser became the first person to reach the site of Vancouver from inland. This belated breakthrough had little impact on the region, though, since Fraser was unable to reach any trade agreements with the coastal tribes and quickly withdrew to his trading posts in the Rockies.

The Salish Indians thus continued to lead a peaceful existence here for many more years before being disrupted by white settlers. In 1808, except for sporadic visits by Russians, Spaniards and Englishmen looking to trade pelts for fabrics and objects from the Orient, the natives were still living according to the traditions handed down to them by their ancestors. In fact, European influence on their lifestyle remained negligible until the mid-19th century, at which point colonization of the territory began slowly.

Development of Natural Resources

In 1818, Great Britain and the United States created the condominium of Oregon, a vast fur-trading zone along the Pacific bounded by California to the south and Alaska to the north. In so doing, these two countries excluded the Russians and the Spanish from this region once and for all. The employees of the North West Company, founded in Montreal in 1784, combed the valley of the Fraser River in search of furs. Not only did they encounter the coastal Indians, whose precious resources they were depleting, but they also had to adapt to the tumultuous waterways of the Rockies, which made travelling by canoe nearly impossible. In 1827, after the Hudson's Bay Company took over the North West Company, a large fur-trading post was founded in Fort Langley, on the shores of the Fraser, some 90 kilometres east of the present site of Vancouver, which would remain untouched for several more decades.

The 49th parallel was designated the border between the United States and British North America in 1846, cutting the hunting territories in half and thereby putting a damper on the Hudson's Bay Company's activities in the region. It wasn't until the gold rush of 1858 that the region experienced another era of prosperity. When nuggets of the precious metal were discovered in the bed of the Fraser, upriver from Fort Langley, a frenzy broke out. In the space of two years, the valley of the golden river attracted thousands of prospectors, and makeshift wooden villages went up overnight. Some came from Eastern Canada, but most, including a large number of Chinese Americans, were from California.

In the end, however, it was contemporary industrialists' growing interest in the region's cedar and fir trees that led to the actual founding of Vancouver. In 1862, Sewell Prescott Moody, originally from Maine (U.S.A), opened the region's first sawmill at the far end of Burrard Inlet, and ensured its success by creating an entire town, known as Moodyville, around it. A second sawmill, called Hastings Mills, opened east of present-day Chinatown in 1865. Two years later, innkeeper Gassy Jack Deighton arrived in the area and set up a saloon near Hastings Mills, providing a place for sawmill workers to slake their thirst. Before long, various service establishments sprang up around the saloon, thus marking the birth of Gastown, later Vancouver's first neighbourhood.

In 1870, the colonial government of British Columbia renamed the nascent town Granville, after the Duke of Granville. The area continued to develop, and the city of Vancouver was officially founded in April 1886. It was renamed in honour of Captain George Vancouver, who made the first hydrographic surveys of the shores of the Strait of Georgia. Unfortunately, a few weeks later, a forest fire swept through the new town, wiping out everything in its way. In barely 20 minutes, Vancouver was reduced to ashes. In those difficult years, local residents were still cut off from the rest of the world, so the town was reconstructed with an eye on the long term. From that point on, Vancouver's buildings, whether of wood or brick, were made to last.

The Umbilical Cord

The end of the gold rush in 1865 led to a number of economic problems for the colony of British Columbia. Due to American protectionism, local industrialists and merchants could not distribute their products in California, while Montreal was too far away and too hard to reach to be a lucrative market. The only favourable outlets, therefore, were the other British colonies on the Pacific, which paved the way for Vancouver's present prosperity. In 1871, British Columbia agreed to join the Canadian Confederation on the condition that a railway line linking it to the eastern part of the country be built.

Recognizing the potential of this gateway to the Pacific, a group of businessmen from Montreal set out to build a transcontinental railway in 1879. Angus, Allan, McIntyre, Strathcona (Smith), Stephen and the other men who joined forces under the Canadian Pacific banner were not thinking small; they wanted to transform Canada, theretofore only a nation in the political sense of the word, into an economically unified power. Canadian Pacific chose Port Moody (formerly Moodyville) as the western terminus of the railway. On July 4, 1886, the first train from Montreal reached Port Moody after a tortuous journey of about 5,000 km. British Columbia was no longer cut off from the rest of the world; from that point on, it was regularly supplied with goods from Europe, Quebec and Ontario, and could export its own raw materials to more lucrative markets.

A few years later, the tracks were extended 20 km to Vancouver in order to link the transcontinental railway to the new port and thereby allow greater access to the Asian market. This change proved momentous for the city, whose population exploded from 2,500 inhabitants in 1886 to over 120,000 in 1911! Many of the Chinese who had come to North America to help build the railroad settled in Vancouver when the project was finished, generating a certain degree of resentment among white residents, who found the new immigrants a little too exotic for their liking. Nevertheless, the Chinese who had worked for Canadian Pacific and the gold mines in the Rockies were soon joined by Asians from Canton, Japan and Tonkin. The city's Chinatown, which grew up between Gastown and

Hastings Mills, eventually became the second largest in North America after San Francisco's.

At the beginning of the 20th century, the city's economic activity gradually shifted from Gastown to the Canadian Pacific Railway yards, located around Granville Street. Within a few years, lovely stone buildings housing banks and department stores sprang up in this area. Nevertheless, most local residents still earned their livelihood from the lumber and fishing industries and lived in makeshift camps on the outskirts of town. In those days, therefore, downtown Vancouver's rapid development was to some extent artificial, based on visions of prosperity that would not be realized for some time yet. In 1913, the city was much like a gangling adolescent in the midst of a growth spurt. It was then that a major economic crisis occurred, putting an end to local optimism for a while. The opening of the Panama Canal (1914) and the end of World War I enabled Vancouver to emerge from this morass, only to sink right back into it during the crash of 1929. During World War II, residents of Japanese descent were interned and their possessions confiscated. Paranoia prevailed over reason, and these second- and sometimes even third-generation Vancouverites were viewed as potential spies.

The New Metropolis of the Pacific

As a result of the Canadian Pacific railway company's strong presence on the West Coast, Vancouverites turned their attention away from the ocean stretched out before them and concentrated instead on their ties with central and eastern Canada. Nevertheless, the city's dual role as a gateway to the Pacific for North Americans and a gateway to America for Asians was already well established, as evidenced by the massive influx of Chinese immigrants from the 19th century onwards and the numerous import-export businesses dealing in silk, tea and porcelain. The name Vancouver has thus been familiar throughout the Pacific zone for over a century. Starting in 1960, a decline in rail transport to the east prompted the city to shift its attention outward and concentrate on its role as a Pacific metropolis.

With the explosive economic growth of places like Japan, Hong Kong, Taiwan, Singapore, the Philippines, Malaysia and

Thailand, especially in regards to exportation, Vancouver's port expanded at lightning speed. Since 1980, it has been the busiest one in the country; 70.7 million tonnes of merchandise were handled here in 1991. Vancouver's pleasant climate and stunning scenery attract large numbers of eastern Canadians looking to improve their quality of life, as well as Asians seeking a new place to live and invest their money. For example, many affluent residents of Hong Kong, anxious about what would happen when their protectorate returned to China in 1997, chose to relocate here.

Thanks to all this new blood, Vancouver (especially the downtown core) has enjoyed continued growth since the late 1960s. Even more than San Francisco or Los Angeles, Vancouver has a strong, positive image throughout the Pacific. It is viewed as a neutral territory offering a good yield on investments and a comfortable standard of living.

The holding of the Asia-Pacific Economic (APEC) summit in Vancouver in November 1997 soilidified Vancouver's position as a key player on the Pacific Rim, and should bolster its status in this market. APEC is a regional consultative body aimed at promoting open trade and economic cooperation between member countries, these include Australia, Brunei, Canada, Chile, China, Hong Kong, Indonesia, Japan, South Korea, Malaysia, Mexico, New Zealand, Papua New Guinea, Philippines, Singapore, Taiwan, Thailand, and the United States.

POPULATION

Vancouver has always been considered the "end of the line" in Canada, the final destination for those looking for a better world. From the era of the steamship to that of the transcontinental railroad, and on to the modern age of the jumbo jet, the city has continued to attract adventurers eager to line their pockets, as well as more philosophical souls looking for peace and a sense of well-being. Located at the edge of a continent that developed from east to west, Vancouver was shrouded in mystery for many years, a sort of Eldorado tinged with Confucianism from the far reaches of the world. These two visions of Vancouver sometimes lead to confrontations between people concerned primarily with economics and developing natural resources and those more interested in ecology. In the end, though, everyone agrees and revels in Vancouver's west-coast way of life.

In 1989, there were 1,471,844 people living in Greater Vancouver; today, there are an estimated 1,720,000. The population has thus grown 14% over the past seven years, illustrating the city's economic vitality and the continued attraction it holds for newcomers. Even early on, Vancouver had a multi-ethnic population, but in the wake of the colonial era, residents of British descent still formed a large majority. A number of Americans came here during the gold rush, and soon after, the first wave of Chinese immigrants established the city's Chinatown, which grew considerably after the completion of the Canadian Pacific railway (1886), a good part of which was built by Asian labourers. Before long, a Japanese community was born, further diversifying the city's "Pacific" profile. Today, Vancouver has over 200,000 residents of Asian descent.

The city's cultural mosaic became that much richer in the 20th century, when immigrants from Europe (especially Germany, Poland, Italy and Greece) began arriving. In 1989, Vancouverites of British descent made up only about 30% of the total population. The French Canadian population, which has always been small in British Columbia, stands at about 29,000 (1986), while the native population has dwindled to 12,000 (1991).

CULTURE

Vancouver's reputation has long been one of a very laid-back city whose beautiful landscape is linked to the "coolness" of its inhabitants living in communion with nature. Started in 1920, the Polar Bear Swim, an annual dip in the cold waters of English Bay on New Year's Day, became one of the rare "sociocultural" events. At the time, skiing, hiking and boating were a part of everyday life and cultural life was practically nonexistent. The people who lived in small communities in the area, reserved their Sundays for hockey or baseball.

Sports are now at the heart of some very outstanding events in Vancouver. Fans devote particular energy to the cause, as spectators at state-of-the-art GM Place stadium and as patrons of bars with giant television screens where they drink beer and munch on spicy chicken wings. On January 14, 1994, when the Vancouver Canucks took part in the Stanley Cup finals, 70,000 people flooded Robson Street and there was even a riot.

PORTRAIT

With an economy based primarily on lumber and fishing, the city lived essentially self-sufficiently until the 1986 Universal Exposition. This was significant for Vancouver's economy and reputation. Previously unknown on a world scale, the city started to attract tourists and investors, especially from Asia. In response to this economic revival, sky-scrapers started popping up that competed in height with the magnificent Art-Deco-style Marine Building and the majestic Hotel Vancouver, built around the same time. Consequently, Vancouver has put a lot of emphasis on architecture, and its most recent addition, the new municipal library, is highly characteristic of the work of its designer, Moshe Safdi. In shape and colour, it is reminiscent of the Roman Coliseum ruins. Tourism has also experienced a lot of growth since Expo '86 and has become an important source of revenue for Vancouver. Cruises to Alaska are one successful example of the city's efforts to develop its tourist industry.

Vancouver's gay community – the largest in Canada – has grown over the years and its vibrancy contributes greatly to making the city more exciting. Many groups have been founded for the purpose of promoting human rights. In terms of culture, the gay community here is very active and heavily involved in the fields of Classical music, singing and visual arts. Joe Average, an HIV-positive painter, is a leading activist among homosexual artists in Vancouver and devotes his life and work to the fight against AIDS.

Because of its geographic location, Vancouver has always been an inspiration to artists, but artistic and cultural activity here has only really started to develop in the last two decades and is slowly becoming more established. Emily Carr (1871-1945), with her relentless desire to depict the natural environment of this isolated area, at a time when there were no means of transportation, was the most striking and encouraging role model for artists who followed. Her paintings are in all of Vancouver's museums along with works by members of the

---

Marker for Change

To commemorate the killing of 14 women at the École Polytechnique in Montréal in 1989, the Women's Monument Committee erected the Marker for Change on Dec. 6, 1997, the eighth anniversary of the massacre. Designed by Torontonian Beth Alber, it features 14 pink-granite benches, each inscribed with the name of one of the victims, that form a circle in Thornton Park in East Vancouver. The monument's dedication to all women killed by men is in seven languages.

Group of Seven, who made landscapes throughout Canada famous. Native art is highly prominent in the area and its two most important representatives are Robert Davidson and, especially, the great sculptor, Bill Reid.

The mixture of various ethnic backgrounds gives Vancouver a distinctive character. The diversity of customs and beliefs is starting to interest more people. Fashion shows and exhibitions are on the rise. Also, Asian immigration brings considerable cultural and economic dynamism. Communities from mainland China, Hong Kong and Taiwan preserve their cultures, which are rich in symbols and events. The Dragon Boat Festival and Chinese New Year are the biggest events, during which Vancouver becomes immersed in Chinese culture for many days.

Cinema has always been a part of daily life in Vancouver. A day doesn't go by when there isn't a film crew on one of Vancouver's streets. Studios have been established in North Vancouver and it's no longer surprising to run into Hollywood stars on the streets or in the shops. Every autumn, the Vancouver International Film Festival offers close to 150 quality foreign films, much to the pleasure of film buffs. The fireworks festival sponsored by Benson & Hedges is a sacred summer ritual. Every year, at the end of July, over 200,000 people serenely make their way to the beaches on English Bay to attend four extraordinary pyrotechnic performances.

Theatre and music are experiencing exceptional growth; sponsors, such as DuMaurier for the Vancouver International

Jazz Festival, offer wonderful opportunities and create the best conditions for both artists and fans. Vancouver is also favoured among writers for the Vancouver Writers Festival, which organized over 40 events last year.

The city is also slowly starting to gain recognition for its many fine restaurants, which are often influenced by various types of international cuisine and offer the added touch of friendly service. Viticulture, or wine growing, is in full expansion. Wine festivals abound, and consumers' tastes are becoming more refined. This cultural explosion, reaching further and further, beyond the borders of British Columbia and even Canada, has been so successful that the United States and Russia chose Vancouver for the Clinton-Yeltsin summit in 1993.

Famous Vancouverites

Vancouver boasts an increasing number of world-famous personalities, particularly in the world of film. Its climate and natural environment, and fiscal conditions that are attractive to American producers have contributed to making such Canadian actors as **Cameron Bancroff, Margot Kidder, Bruce Greenwood** and **Cynthia Stevenson** known to the public. American stars such as **Christopher Reeve**, who starred in *Superman*, **Mel Gibson**, featured in *Bird On A Wire*, which was shot in the streets of Gastown, and **Jackie Chan**, who shook the downtown area in *Rumble in the Bronx*, have also been captivated by Vancouver's charm. The list hardly ends here as **Robert DeNiro, Goldie Hawn, Charlton Heston** and many others have shot movies in the streets of Vancouver. Moreover, *The X Files* is a "made in Vancouver" production (for now). Another anecdote: **Pamela Anderson**, the sexy star of *Baywatch*, is also from Vancouver.

Bryan Adams

This rock superstar has sold over 45 million records throughout the world. He comes from West Vancouver, where he still has a house. He returns occasionally to record songs and sign autographs.

Joe Average

He is a contemporary figurative artist, using bright colours in his work. His posters can be seen throughout the city, and one of these was used as official promotion for the International Conference on AIDS. He decided to dedicate his art to the cause of AIDS upon being diagnosed as HIV positive.

Dave Barr

This Vancouver golfer has been taking part in international tournaments for 20 years. Born in Kelowna, in the Okanagan Valley, he began his career in 1974 and has represented Canada 13 times at the World Cup, winning it twice.

Niels Bendtsen

Another famous Vancouverite, Niels Bendtsen is a furniture designer whose art has transcended national boundaries. His work is on permanent display at the New York Museum of Modern Art, and his output extends all the way to Europe. Closer to home, he designed the interior layout of the Starbucks coffee shops.

George Bowering

This major literary personality from Vancouver became famous in the sixties as the founder and editor in chief of *Tish* magazine. His reputation has been growing ever since. An English professor at SFU, he has written and published over 40 books of poetry, fiction and history, and has received the Governor General's Award on three occasions.

Jay Brazeau

This Vancouver actor attracted notice in the well-known television series *We're No Angels* and *The X Files*. He has also worked in radio and received three Jessie Awards. Leading actor in the recent film *Kissed*, he remains part of the current film scene.

PORTRAIT

Pavel Bure

Nicknamed the Russian Rocket, he is considered the most promising hockey player on the continent. This Canucks superstar has scored 60 goals in two consecutive seasons.

Glen Clark

Glen Clark is the Premier of British Columbia. This young and charming politician is the leader of the provincial New Democratic Party (NDP), a "left-of-centre" party. He did his best to dispel acknowledged hostilities toward socialism and distinguished himself by taking a firm stand against American policy as regards commercial fishing. He won the provincial elections for the second time in 1996.

Kim Campbell

She was Canada's first female Prime Minister, but was not re-elected. In 1996, she was named Consul General of Canada in Los Angeles.

James Chong

A very wealthy architect born in Hong Kong, he has become the darling of Vancouver. He is currently focusing on the construction of large buildings, giving precedence to quality of life and the environment.

Douglas Coupland

The man who coined the term Generation X is another famous Vancouverite. He currently lives on the side of the North Shore Mountains and resurfaces every now and then to put in his two cents worth on the future of Canada, British Columbia and of course Vancouver. He underlines the idea that Vancouver's geography alone distinguishes it tremendously from the rest of Canada, that it is developing an identity quite apart from the other major Canadian cities (see also p 188).

Sam Feldman

Through his dynamism, will and talent as a talent agent, he is now involved in all North-American musical productions and film scores. He represents 150 artists, including Bryan Adams.

Jim Pattison

Jim Pattison is without a doubt the most powerful and respected businessman in Vancouver. He is also the wealthiest. His companies employ 17,000 people and make between three and four billion dollars in annual sales.

Sarah McLachlan

Born in Halifax, Nova Scotia, Sarah McLachlan nevertheless considers herself a Vancouver artist, it may have something to do with the fact that her record label is the Vancouver-based Nettwerk. Fans appreciate her ethereal voice and emotional and forthright songs and her latest album, *Surfacing*, is already a success. Lillith Fair, the all-female musical tour conceived by McLachlan that, as she puts it, "doesn't exclude men" but "simply celebrates women", has made her one of the most well-known female performers in North America.

Bill Reid

Established in Vancouver, this great sculptor has been representing the art of his Haida ancestors with much influence and skill since 1940. His sculptures can be seen all over the city as well as at the UBC Museum of Anthropology and the Vancouver Art Gallery. Two of his works not be missed are the one at the Aquarium and the magnificent sculpture at the Vancouver airport.

Paul Watson

Co-founder of Greenpeace, he is now president of the Sea Shepherd Conservation Society, which protects the environment and, more particularly, the waters and their fauna.

He has often come under criticism, and his methods have been compared to those of an "eco-terrorist".

ARCHITECTURE

Vancouver was founded during an era of eager westward expansion. Within a few months in 1865, scores of wooden buildings sprang up here, providing the employees of the area's newly opened sawmills with places to sleep, purchase goods and entertain themselves. The vast majority of these makeshift structures fell victim either to the wear and tear of time or the devastating fire of 1886, which destroyed a large part of the young city. You can see one of the few buildings that has survived from that era in Pioneer Park (see p 108).

In the years following the fire, the centre of town, located in what is now Gastown, was reconstructed out of brick in order to prevent destruction of the growing city by another blaze. Although the earliest buildings of that era were modelled after the Italianate architecture that had enjoyed such great popularity on the east coast two decades prior (prominent cornices, small pediments over doors and windows), Vancouver caught up quickly, adopting Richardson's neo-Romanesque style, as other cities all over North America had done. This style, inspired by French Romanesque art, was reinterpreted by Boston architect Henry Hobson Richardson, who designed massive, robust-looking structures with large, arched openings. Other late 19th-century buildings have more in common with the vernacular architecture of San Francisco (multi-level oriel windows overhanging sidewalks, projecting cornices), evidence of Vancouver's close ties with the rest of the west coast.

At the beginning of the 20th century, Vancouver experienced a period of phenomenal growth. Entire neighbourhoods sprang up in a single summer. In most residential areas, wood was the material of choice, since it was inexpensive and available in large quantities. The risks of fire, furthermore, were minimal, as the houses were almost all free-standing. Space was not a problem, so San Francisco's Queen Anne style, characterized by numerous gables and turrets, was used for these homes. Downtown, brick slowly gave way to stone, a richer material, for proud Vancouverites were eager to show the rest of the world that they were dynamic and urbane. It is for that reason that the largest skyscraper in the British Empire (see Sun Tower, p 70) was built in Vancouver, rather than in Toronto or London, in 1912. Next, Canadian Pacific introduced the Château style to Vancouver, along with the Beaux-Arts style and its offshoots, neo-Classical revival and baroque revival, which are all well represented here. The Chinese community also made a significant contribution to the city's architecture, building narrow commercial buildings with deep loggias and parapets on top, reflecting an interesting blend of North American and Asian styles.

Starting in 1913, Vancouver experienced a growth slump, from which it did not truly recover until after the Second World War. Consequently, few new buildings went up in the twenties and thirties. You will nevertheless find a few examples of the Art Deco style here, including the Marine Building, which faces straight down West Hastings Street (see p 76) and is viewed as one of the landmarks of the business district.

As Vancouver is a thriving young city, its architecture is predominantly modern and post-modern. Thanks to talented architects who are open to experimentation and a cultural climate that combines innovative Californian influences with the traditional building techniques of China, Japan and even some of British Columbia's native communities, the city has developed an exceptional and modern architectural heritage since the 1940s.

From the glass and steel skyscrapers downtown to the houses clinging to mountainsides in North and West Vancouver, with their simple post-and-beam construction, the accent is usually on purity of line. This sober, sophisticated style contrasts sharply with the ostentation of the early part of the century... and to a certain extent that of contemporary, late 20th-century architecture as well. Indeed, since the emergence of post-modernism, there has been a shift back to the lavish forms of the past. Many recent immigrants favour columns and decorated pediments, which they proudly photograph for their families back home. In some areas, furthermore, houses built in the fifties and sixties are being replaced by what Vancouverites have termed "monster-houses", giant structures that take up almost their entire plot of land, usurping space once occupied by trees and gardens.

PRACTICAL INFORMATION

 nformation in this chapter will help visitors better plan their trip to Vancouver.

ENTRANCE FORMALITIES

Passport

For a stay of less than three months in Canada, a valid passport is usually sufficient for most visitors and a visa is not required. American residents do not need passports, though these are the best form of identification. A three-month extension is possible, but a return ticket and proof of sufficient funds to cover this extension may be required.

Caution: some countries do not have an agreement with Canada concerning health and accident insurance, so it is advisable to have the appropriate coverage. For more information, see the section entitled, "Health", on page 50.

Canadian citizens who wish to enter the United States, to visit Alaska or Washington State for example, do not need visas, neither do citizens of the majority of Western European countries. A valid passport is sufficient for a stay of less than three months. A return ticket and proof of sufficient funds to cover your stay may be required.

Extended Visits

A visitor must submit a request to extend his or her visit **in writing**, **before** the expiration of his or her visa (the date is usually written in your passport) to an Immigration Canada office. To make a request you must have a valid passport, a return ticket, proof of sufficient funds to cover the stay, as well as the $65 non-refundable filing-fee. In some cases (work, study), however, the request must be made **before** arriving in Canada.

CUSTOMS

If you are bringing gifts into Canada, remember that certain restrictions apply.

Smokers (minimum age is 16) can bring in a maximum of 200 cigarettes, 50 cigars, 400 grams of tobacco, or 400 tobacco sticks.

For wine and alcohol the limit is 1.1 litres; in practice, however, two bottles per person are usually allowed. The limit for beer is twenty-four 355-ml size cans or bottles.

Plants, vegetation, and food: there are very strict rules regarding the importation of plants, flowers, and other vegetation; it is therefore not advisable to bring any of these types of products into the country. If it is absolutely necessary, contact the Customs-Agriculture service of the Canadian embassy **before** leaving your country.

Pets: if you are travelling with your pet, you will need a health certificate (available from your veterinarian) as well as a rabies vaccination certificate. It is important to remember that the vaccination must have been administered **at least 30 days before** your departure and should not be more than a year old.

Tax reimbursements for visitors: it is possible to be reimbursed for certain taxes paid on purchases made in Canada (see p 59).

EMBASSIES AND CONSULATES

Canadian Embassies and Consulates Abroad

Australia
Canadian Consulate General, Level 5, Quay West, 111 Harrington Road, Sydney, N.S.W., Australia 2000, ☎ (612) 364-3000, ⊷ (612) 364-3098

Belgium
Canadian Embassy, 2 Avenue de Tervueren, 1040 Brussels, ☎ (2) 735.60.40, ⊷ (2) 732.67.90

Denmark
Canadian Embassy, Kr. Bernikowsgade 1, DK = 1105 Copenhagen K, Denmark, ☎ (45) 12.22.99, ⊷ (45) 14.05.85

Finland
Canadian Embassy, Pohjos Esplanadi 25 B, 00100 Helsinki, Finland, ☎ (9) 171-141, ⊷ (9) 601-060

Germany
Canadian Consulate General, Internationales, Handelzentrum, Friedrichstrasse 95, 23rd Floor, 10117 Berlin, Germany, ☎ (30) 261.11.61, ⊷ (30) 262.92.06

Great Britain
Canada High Commission, Macdonald House, One Grosvenor Square, London W1X 0AB, England
☎ (171) 258-6600, ⊷ (171) 258-6384

Italy
Canadian Embassy, Via G.B. de Rossi 27, 00161 Rome, ☎ (6) 44.59.81, ⊷ (6) 44.59.87

Netherlands
Canadian Embassy, Parkstraat 25, 2514JD The Hague, Netherlands, ☎ (70) 361-4111, ⊷ (70) 365-6283

Norway
Canadian Embassy, Oscars Gate 20, Oslo 3, Norway, ☎ (47) 46.69.55, ✉ (47) 69.34.67

Spain
Canadian Embassy, Edificio Goya, Calle Nunez de Balboa 35, 28001 Madrid, ☎ (1) 431.43.00, ✉ (1) 431.23.67

Sweden
Canadian Embassy, Tegelbacken 4, 7th floor, Stockholm, Sweden, ☎ (8) 613-9900, ✉ (8) 24.24.91

Switzerland
Canadian Embassy, Kirchenfeldstrasse 88, 3000 Berne 6, ☎ (31) 532.63.81, ✉ (31) 352.73.15

United States
Canadian Embassy, 501 Pennsylvania Avenue NW, Washington, DC, 20001, ☎ (202) 682-1740, ✉ (202) 682-7726

Canadian Consulate General, Suite 400 South Tower, One CNN Center, Atlanta, Georgia, 30303-2705, ☎ (404) 577-6810 or 577-1512, ✉ (404) 524-5046

Canadian Consulate General, Three Copley Place, Suite 400, Boston, Massachusetts, 02116, ☎ (617) 262-3760, ✉ (617) 262-3415

Canadian Consulate General, Two Prudential Plaza, 180 N. Stetson Avenue, Suite 2400, Chicago, Illinois, 60601, ☎ (312) 616-1860, ✉ (312) 616-1877

Canadian Consulate General, St. Paul Place, Suite 1700, 750 N. St. Paul Street, Dallas, Texas, 75201, ☎ (214) 922-9806, ✉ (214) 922-9815

Canadian Consulate General, 600 Renaissance Center, Suite 1100, Detroit, Michigan, 48234-1798, ☎ (313) 567-2085, ✉ (313) 567-2164

Canadian Consulate General, 300 South Grande Avenue, 10th Floor, California Plaza, Los Angeles, California, 90071, ☎ (213) 687-7432, ✉ (213) 620-8827

Canadian Consulate General, Suite 900, 701 Fourth Avenue South, Minneapolis, Minnesota, 55415-1899, ☎ (612) 333-4641, ⇌ (612) 332-4061

Canadian Consulate General, 1251 Avenue of the Americas, New York, New York, 10020-1175, ☎ (212) 596-1600, ⇌ (212) 596-1793

Canadian Consulate General, One Marine Midland Center, Suite 3000, Buffalo, New York, 14203-2884, ☎ (716) 852-1247, ⇌ (716) 852-4340

Canadian Consulate General, 412 Plaza 600, Sixth and Stewart Streets, Seattle, Washington, 98101-1286, ☎ (206) 442-1777, ⇌ (206) 443-1782

Foreign Consulates in Vancouver

Australian Consulate: 999 Canada Place, Suite 602, Vancouver, BC, V6C 3E1, ☎ (604) 684-1177,

Honorary Consulate of Belgium: Birks Place, Suite 570, 688 West Hastings, Vancouver, BC, V6B 1P4, ☎ (604) 684-6838

British Consulate General: 111 Melville St., Suite 800, Vancouver, BC, V6E 3V6, ☎ (604) 683-4421

Consulate General of Germany: World Trade Centre, 999 Canada Place, Suite 704, Vancouver, BC, V6C 3E1, ☎ (604) 684-8377

Consulate General of Italy: 1200 Burrard Street, Suite 705, Vancouver, B.C., V6Z 2C7, ☎ (604) 684-7288, ⇌ (604) 685-4263

Consulate General of the Netherlands: 475 Howe Street, Suite 821, Vancouver, BC, V6C 2B3, ☎ (604) 684-6448

Consulate General of Spain: There is no Spanish consulate in Vancouver. If you have any inquiries, contact the consulate general in Toronto: 1200 Bay Street, Suite 400, Toronto, Ont., M5R 2A5, ☎ (416) 967-4949, ⇌ (416) 925-4949

PRACTICAL INFORMATION

Consulate General of Switzerland 999 Canada Place, Suite 790, Vancouver, BC, V6C 3E1, ☎ (604) 684-2231

U.S. Consulate General 1095 West Pender, Vancouver, BC, V6E 2M6, ☎ (604) 685-4311

 TOURIST INFORMATION

The Tourism **Vancouver Tourist Info Centre** *(May to Sep, every day 8am to 6pm; Sep to May, Mon to Fri 8:20am to 5pm, Sat 9am to 5pm; Plaza Level, Waterfront Centre, 200 Burrard St., V6C 3L6, ☎ 683-2000)* provides brochures and information on sights and accommodations for the city as well as for the province.

For information on and reservations for travelling in the rest of the province you can call **Super, Natural British Columbia** at ☎ 1-800-663-6000 or write to them at Box 9830, Station Province-Government, Victoria, V8W 9W5.

Vancouver Parks & Recreation: ☎ 257-8400. Provides all information on sports and recreation activities.

Calendar of Sports and Cultural Events (24 hours/day): ☎ 661-7373

For information on Vancouver and British Columbia on the internet, check out the following sites:

Tourism Vancouver *(☎ 683-2000)* www.tourism-vancouver.org
In Vancouver! www.vancouver-bc.com
Excite Travel www.city.net/countries/canada/british_columbia/
Super, Natural British Columbia www.travel.bc.ca

The **Canada Tourism Commission** *(62-65 Trafalgar Square, London WC2N 5DT, public enquiries ☎ 0891 715000 (premium rate), ⊷ 0171 389 1149, e-mail vcc@dial.pipex.com)* can provide general tourist information for the whole country.

GUIDED TOURS

Guided tours of all sorts are available to help you discover every facet of Vancouver.

The **Gastown Business Improvement Society** *(☎ 683-5650)* offers free walking tours of Gastown once a day during the months of June, July and August. Tours last about two hours.

Gray Line of Vancouver *(☎ 879-3363 or 1-800-667-0882)* offers city tours year-round aboard comfortable buses. The tour lasts three and a half hours and costs $38.50 for adults and $27 for children. In the summer, they also offer a shorter double-decker tour. You can get on and off as you please and the cost is $22 for adults and $11 for children. The route is posted in the lobbies of most downtown hotels and the entire tour takes about two hours. You must purchase your ticket ahead of time, either by calling the above numbers or by visiting the agent in the lobby of the Hotel Vancouver (see p 146). Gray Line also offers excursions to Victoria and Whistler

The **Vancouver Trolley Company Ltd.** *(☎ 451-5581 or 1-888-451-5581)*toots around town in a old-fashioned trolleys, picking up and dropping off passengers as they wish at 16 different stops, and providing narration the whole way.

Harbour Cruises Ltd. *(☎ 688-7246 or 1-800-663-1500)* organizes narrated boat tours of the Inner Harbour, that last about 90 minutes and depart three times daily. The cost is $16 for adults and $5 for children. They also offer sunset dinner cruises which feature a buffet meal and a trip out to English Bay and False Creek. This is a great way to experience this city set between sea and sky.

Stanley Park Horse Drawn Tours *(☎ 681-5116)* offers hour-long jaunts through beautiful Stanley Park. Your carriage awaits at the information booth at the lower zoo parking lot every day from March to October. There are departures every 20 to 30 minutes and the cost is $10 for adults and $6 for children.

PRACTICAL INFORMATION

West Coast City and Nature Sightseeing Tours *(☎ 451-1600)* has multilingual guides and offers minibus tours year round. Destinations include Whistler, Capilano and Butchart Gardens.

 ## FINDING YOUR WAY AROUND

The area code is 604

By Plane

From Europe

There are two possibilities: direct flights or flights with a stopover in Montreal, Toronto or Calgary. Direct flights are of course much more attractive since they are considerably faster than flights with a stopover (for example expect about nine hours from Amsterdam for a direct flight compared to 13 hours). In some cases, however, particularly if you have a lot of time, it can be advantageous to combine a charter flight from Europe with one of the many charter flights within Canada from either Montreal or Toronto. Prices for this option can vary considerably depending on whether you are travelling during high or low season.

At press time, five airline companies offered direct flights from Europe to Vancouver.

Air Canada offers daily direct flights during the summer from Paris to Vancouver and from London to Vancouver. Air Canada also flies twice a week from Frankfurt to Vancouver. **Canadian Airlines** offers direct flights from London to Vancouver, as well as direct flights from Frankfurt to Vancouver.

KLM offers a direct flight from Amsterdam to Vancouver three times a week.

Lufthansa offers a daily flight in partnership with Canadian Airlines from Frankfurt to Vancouver.

British Airways offers daily non-stop service from London to Vancouver.

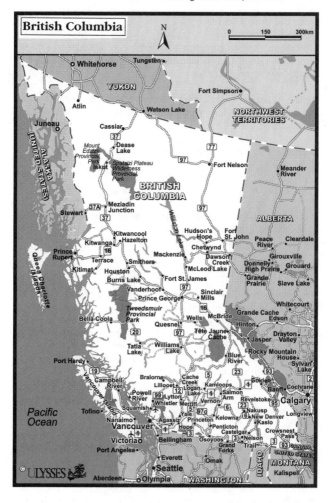

From the United States

Travellers arriving from the southern or southeastern United States may want to consider **American Airlines** which flies into Vancouver through Dallas.

Delta Airlines offers direct flights from Los Angeles to Vancouver. Travellers from the eastern United States go through Salt Lake City.

Northwest Airlines flies into Vancouver via Minneapolis.

From Asia

Both **Air Canada** and **Canadian Airlines** offer direct flights between Vancouver and Hong Kong.

Within Canada

Air Canada and **Canadian Airlines** are the only companies that offer regular flights to Vancouver within Canada. Daily flights to Vancouver as well as many other cities are offered from all the major cities in the country. Flights from Eastern Canada often have stopovers in Montreal or Toronto. For example Air Canada flies to Vancouver 14 times a week. During the high season, the aforementioned flights are complemented by many others offered by charter companies, including Air Transat, Royal and Canada 3000. These flights are subject to change with respect to availability and fares.

Air Canada's regional partner **Air BC** offers flights within British Columbia, as does Canadian Airlines' regional partner, **Canadian Regional**.

Harbour Air Seaplanes *(☎ 688-1277 or 1-800-665-0212 or 384-2215, in Victoria, ≈ 278-5271)* offers scheduled flights to Victoria, the Gulf Islands and northern British Columbia.

Helijet Airways *(☎ 273-1414 or 1-800-665-4354, ≈ 273-5301)* provides scheduled helicopter service to Victoria and Seattle.

Airlines (information and reservations)

Air Canada, ☎ 688-5515
Air China, ☎ 685-0921
Air France, ☎ 1-800-667-2747
American Airlines, ☎ 1-800-433-7300
Canadian Airlines, ☎ 279-6611
Canadian Helicopters, ☎ 278-5502
Cathay Pacific, ☎ 606-8888
Continental Airlines, ☎ 1-800-231-0856
Delta Airlines, ☎ 1-800-221-1212
Harbour Air, ☎ 688-1277
Horizon Air, ☎ 1-800-547-9308
Japan Airlines, ☎ 1-800-525-3663
KLM Royal Dutch, ☎ 279-5433
Lufthansa German Airline, ☎ 1-800-563-5459
Quantas Airways, ☎ 1-800-227-4500
United Airlines, ☎ 1-800-241-6522

PRACTICAL INFORMATION

Airport

Vancouver International Airport *(☎ 276-6101)* is served by flights from across Canada, the United States, Europe and Asia. Nineteen airline companies presently use the airport. The airport is located 15 km from downtown.

It takes about 30 minutes to get downtown by car or bus. A taxi or limousine will cost you about $25-$30, or you can take the **Airport Express Bus** *(☎ 244-9888)* which offers shuttle service to the major downtown hotels and the bus depot. The cost is $9 one-way or $15 return for adults. The bus leaves every 15 minutes and runs from 6:30am to 12:10am. To reach downtown by public transit take bus #100 for downtown and points east and bus #404 or #406 for Richmond, Delta and points south. The fare ranges from $1.50 and $3 depending on the time of day and destination.

Air Limo: ☎ 273-1331; limousine to the airport: $29; 20 to 40 minutes journey time.

Take note: even if you have already paid various taxes included in the purchase price of your ticket, Vancouver International

Airport charges every passenger an **Airport Improvement Fee** (AIF). The fee is $5 for flights within B.C. and to the Yukon, $10 for flights elsewhere in North America, and $15 for overseas flights; credit cards are accepted, and most in-transit passengers are exempted.

Besides the regular airport services (duty-free shops, cafeterias, restaurants, etc.) you will also find an exchange office. Several car rental companies also have offices in the airport, including Avis, Thrifty, ABC Rent-a-Car, Budget (see p 46).

By Train

Travellers with a lot of time may want to consider the train, one of the most pleasant and impressive ways to discover Western Canada and reach Vancouver. Via Rail Canada is the only company that offers train travel between the Canadian provinces. This mode of transportation can be combined with air travel (various packages are offered by Air Canada and Canadian Airlines) or on its own from big cities in Eastern Canada like Toronto or Montreal. This last option does require a lot of time however, it takes a minimum of five days to get from Montreal to Vancouver.

The **CanRailpass** is another particularly interesting option. Besides the advantageous price, you only need to purchase one ticket for travel throughout Canada. The ticket allows 12 days of unlimited travel in a 30-day period. At press-time the CanRailpass was $569 in the high season and $369 in the low season (Jan 1 to May 31 and Oct 16 to Dec 31). CanRailpass holders are also entitled to special rates for car rentals.

Via Rail offers several discounts:

Reductions for certain days of the week, during the off-season and on reservations made at least five days in advance: up to 40% off depending on the destination;

Discount for students and those 24 years of age or less: 10% throughout the year or 40% if the reservation is made five days in advance, except during the holidays;

Discount for people aged 60 and over: 10% on certain days during off-peak travel times;

Special rates for children: children two to 11 travel for half-price; children under two accompanied by an adult travel free;

Finally, take note that first-class service is quite exceptional, including a meal, wine, and alcoholic beverages free of charge.

For further information on Via Trains:

Internet: www.viarail.ca

In Canada: ☎ 1-800-561-8630 or contact your travel agent.
In Australia: Walshes World, ☎ (02) 9318 1044, ⇌ (02) 9318 2753.
In Italy: Gastaldi Tours, ☎ (10) 24 511, ⇌ (10) 28 0354.
In the Netherlands: Incento B.V., ☎ (035) 69 55111, ⇌ (035) 69 55155.
In New Zealand: Walshes World, ☎ (09) 379-3708, ⇌ (09) 309 0725.
In Switzerland: Touring Club Suisse, ☎ (22) 737 1313, ⇌ (22) 737 1590.
In the United Kingdom: Leisurail, ☎ 01733-335-599, ⇌ 01733-505-451, or Airsavers at ☎ 0141-303-0308, ⇌ 041-303-0306.
In the United States: ☎ 1-800-561-3949 or contact Amtrak or your travel agent.

Trains from the United States and Eastern Canada arrive at the new intermodal **Pacific Central Station** *(Via Rail Canada, 1150 Station St., ☎ 1-800-561-8630)* where you can also connect to buses or the surface public transportation system known as the **Skytrain**. The cross-country Via train, **The Canadian** arrives in Vancouver three times a week from Eastern Canada. The trip from Edmonton to Vancouver is a spectacular trip through the mountains along the rivers and valleys. Those in a rush should keep in mind that the trip takes 24 hours, and is more of a tourist excursion than a means of transportation. It costs less that $200 one-way; check with Via, however about seasonal rates.

BC Rail *(1311 W. 1st St., North Vancouver, ☎ 984-5246)* trains travel the northern west coast. Schedules vary depending on the seasons.

During the summer, the **Great Canadian Railtour Company Ltd.** offers **Rocky Mountain Railtours** *($700 per person, $645 per person double occupancy; ☎ 606-7200 or 1-800-665-7245, ☎ 606-7520)* between Calgary and Vancouver.

There is daily service aboard **Amtrak's Mount Baker International** from Seattle, Washington; the trip takes three hours and follows a scenic route. For reservations or information call Amtrak US Rail at 1-800-USA-RAIL or 1-800-872-7245 (toll-free in North America).

Train Rides

The railway enabled Vancouver to open up to the rest of Canada. Due to the province's very steep terrain, some routes are still considered reckless, defying the very laws of engineering. These first-class local trains still run, travelling to regions and **landscapes** that would otherwise be inaccessible. All departures from Vancouver.

The **Royal Hudson** *(1311 W. 1st St., North Vancouver, ☎ 631-3500)* steam locomotive is very well-known in Vancouver tourist circles. Dating from the beginning of the century, but restored, it takes passengers from its station in North Vancouver to Squamish, 65 kilometres away. The journey allows passengers to discover the splendid **Howe Sound** fjord, as the railway skirts the shore.

Rocky Mountain Railtours *(1150 Station St., Vancouver, ☎ 606-7200)*. This agency's very comfortable train with vast carriages offering panoramic views will take you to the **Rockies** for several days. An extraordinary experience.

For more information on railways radiating around Vancouver: **VIA Rail Canada**, ☎ 1-800-561-8630.

By Ferry

Two ferry ports serve the greater Vancouver area for travellers coming from other regions in the province. Horseshoe Bay, to the northwest, is the terminal for ferries to Nanaimo (crossing time 90 minutes), Bowen Island and the Mainland Sunshine Coast. Tsawwassen, to the south, is the terminal for ferries to Victoria (Swartz Bay) (crossing time 95 minutes), Nanaimo (crossing time two hours) and the Southern Gulf Islands. Both terminals are about 30 minutes from downtown. For information on these routes contact the **BC Ferries** *(☎ 1-888-BCFERRY, 250-386-3431 or 669-1211).*

By Bus

The new intermodal **Pacific Central Station** was opened in 1993 in the old Via Station to allow travellers to connect between bus, train and public transportation in one place. Buses provide several links with the main cities in the province.

Greyhound Lines of Canada: Pacific Central Station, 1150 Station St., ☎ 482-8747 or 1-800-661-8747.

Maverick Coach Lines (☎ 662-8051) offers service to Nanaimo, and **Pacific Coach Lines** (☎ 662-8074) to Victoria.

West Coast Express: ☎ 683-RAIL
Vancouver Main Bus Station: ☎ 683-8133
Pacific Coach Lines (to Victoria): ☎ 662-8074

By Car

Vancouver is accessible by the **TransCanada Highway 1**, which runs east-west. This national highway links all of the major Canadian cities. It has no tolls and passes through some spectacular scenery. Coming from Alberta you will pass through the Rocky Mountains, desert regions and a breathtaking canyon.

PRACTICAL INFORMATION

Table of Distances (km/mi)						© ULYSSES
By the shortest route						
				Calgary (Alberta)		Calgary (Alberta)
			Edmonton (Alberta)	278/173		Edmonton (Alberta)
		Harrison Hot Springs	1147/713	869/540		Harrison Hot Springs
	Jasper (Alberta)	893/555	365/227	408/254		Jasper (Alberta)
Seattle (Washington)	1128/701	247/153	1364/848	1086/675		Seattle (Washington)
Vancouver	226/140	794/493	125/78	1155/718	967/606	Vancouver
Whistler	123/76	350/217	949/590	256/159	1186/737	907/564	Whistler

1 mile = 1.6 kilometres	Example :	The distance between Edmonton and
1 kilometre = 0.62 mile		Vancouver is 1155 km or 718 mi.

The city is generally reached from the east by taking the "Downtown" exit from the TransCanada. If you are coming from the United States or from Victoria by ferry, you will enter the city on Highway 99 North; in this case expect it to take about 30 minutes to reach downtown.

Driver's licenses from Western European countries are valid in Canada and the United States. While North American travellers won't have any trouble adapting to the rules of the road in Western Canada, European travellers may need a bit more time to get used to things. Here are a few hints:

Rules of the Road

Drivers in Western Canada are particularly courteous when it comes to **pedestrians**, and willingly stop to give them the right of way even in big cities, so as a driver keep an eye out for pedestrians. Pedestrian crosswalks are usually indicated by a yellow sign.

Turning **right on a red light** when the way is clear is permitted in British Columbia.

When a **school bus** (usually yellow in colour) has stopped and has its signals flashing, you must come to a complete stop, no matter what direction you are travelling in. Failing to stop at the flashing signals is considered a serious offense, and carries a heavy penalty.

Wearing of **seatbelts** in the front and back seats is mandatory at all times.

Almost all highways in Western Canada are toll-free, and just a few bridges have tolls. The **speed limit** on highways is 100 km/h. The speed limit on secondary highways is 90 km/h, and 50 km/h in urban areas.

Because Canada produces its own crude oil, **gasoline** (petrol) prices are much less expensive than in Europe, and only slightly more than in the United States. Some gas stations (especially in the downtown areas) might ask for payment in advance as a security measure, especially after 11pm.

Accidents and Emergencies

In case of serious accident, fire or other emergency dial ☎ **911** or **0**.

If you run into trouble on the highway, pull onto the shoulder of the road and turn the hazard lights on. If it is a rental car, contact the rental company as soon as possible. Always file an accident report. If a disagreement arises over who was at fault in an accident, ask for police help.

FINDING YOUR WAY AROUND THE CITY

By Car

Driving in the City

Getting around Vancouver by car is easy; take note, however, that the government has decided not to build any expressways through downtown, which is exceptional for a city of 1.7 million people; as a result rush-hour traffic can be quite heavy. If you have the time, by all means explore the city on foot.

Car Rentals

Packages including air travel, hotel and car rental or just hotel and car rental are often less expensive than car rental alone. It is best to shop around. Remember also that some companies offer corporate rates and discounts to auto-club members. Some travel agencies work with major car rental companies (Avis, Budget, Hertz, etc.) and offer good values; contracts often include added bonuses (reduced ticket prices for shows, etc.).

When renting a car, find out if the contract includes unlimited kilometres, and if the insurance provides full coverage (accident, property damage, hospital costs for you and passengers, theft).

Certain credit cards, gold cards for example, cover the collision and theft insurance. Check with your credit card company before renting.

To rent a car you must be at least 21 years of age and have had a driver's license for **at least** one year. If you are between 21 and 25, certain companies (for example Avis, Thrifty, Budget) will ask for a $500 deposit, and in some cases they will also charge an extra sum for each day you rent the car. These conditions do not apply for those over 25 years of age.

A credit card is extremely useful for the deposit to avoid tying up large sums of money.

Most rental cars come with an automatic transmission, however you can request a car with a manual shift.

Child safety seats cost extra.

Car Rental Companies

You can rent a car at the airport or in the city.

Downtown:

Tilden: 1128 W. Georgia St., ☎ 685-6111, 1-800-227-7368 or 1-800-CAR-RENT or at the airport ☎ 273-3121

Budget: 450 W. Georgia St., and at the airport ☎ 668-7000 or 1-800-268-8900 (from Canada) or 1-800-527-0700 (from the US)

ABC Rent-a-Car: 255 W. Broadway, ☎ 873-6622 or 1-800-464-6422

Thrifty: 1400 Robson St., ☎ 681-4869 or at the airport ☎ 276-0800

Avis: 757 Hornby St., ☎ 606-2847 or at the airport ☎ 606-2847

Exotic Car and Motorcycle Rentals: 1820 Burrard St., ☎ 736-9130 or 644-9128

Scooter Metro Rentals: 1610 Robson Street, ☎ 685-0099; rents bicycles, scooters and motorcycles by the hour, half-day or day.

Dollar Rent-a-Car: ☎ 1-800-800-4000

Lo-Cost Rent-a-Car: ☎ 689-9664

PRACTICAL INFORMATION

By Taxi

Hailing a taxi in Vancouver is not a problem, especially near the entrances of big downtown hotels and along main arteries such as Robson Street and Georgia Street. The main taxi companies are:

Yellow Cab: ☎ 681-1111
McLure's: ☎ 731-9211
Black Top: ☎ 731-1111, 871-1111 (wheelchair accessible taxis).
For limousines: ☎ 582-5544 or 671-5733

Public Transportation

BC Transit bus route maps are available from the Vancouver Travel InfoCentre *(summer, every day 8am to 6pm; rest of the year, Mon to Fri 8:30am to 5pm, Sat 9am to 5pm; 200 Burrard St., ☎ 683-2000)* or from the BC Transit offices in Surrey *(13401 108th Ave., 5th floor, Surrey, B.C., ☎ 1-800-903-4731 or 540-3450)*, which is located.

BC Transit also includes a rail transit system and a marine bus. The **Skytrain** runs east from the downtown area to Burnaby,

New Westminster and Surrey. These automatic trains run from 5am to 1am all week, except Sundays when they start at 9am. The **Seabus** shuttles frequently between Burrard Inlet and North Vancouver.

Tickets and passes are available for **BC Transit**, including Skytrain and Seabus tickets from the coin-operated machines at some stops, in some convenience stores or by calling ☎ 261-5100 or 521-0400.

The fares are the same whether you are travelling on a BC Transit bus, the Skytrain or the Seabus. A single ticket generally costs $1.50 for adults and $0.75 for seniors, children and students (must have BC Transit GoCard), except at peak hours (Mon to Fri before 9:30am and 3pm to 6:30pm) when the system is divided into three zones and it costs $1.50 for travel within one zone, $2.25 within two zones and $3 within three zones.

BC Transit lost and found: ☎ 682-7887.

West Vancouver is served by the **Blue Bus** *(☎ 985-7777)*.

Car & Van Pooling: ☎ 879-RIDE

Handicapped Transportation

Handydart *(300-3200 E. 54th St., ☎ 430-2692)* provides public transportation for wheelchair-bound individuals. You must reserve your seat in advance.

Vancouver Taxis *(2205 Main St., ☎ 255-5111 or 874-5111)* also offers transportation for handicapped individuals.

On Foot

The best way to truly appreciate the many facets of any city is generally by foot. This guide outlines nine walking tours in different neighbourhoods. Don't forget your walking shoes!

Drivers in Vancouver are particularly courteous when it comes to **pedestrians**, and willingly stop to give them the right of way even in big cities, so be careful when and where you step off the curb. Pedestrian crosswalks are usually indicated by a yellow sign. When driving pay special attention that there is no one about to cross near these signs.

By Ferry

There is a ferry between Granville Island and the Hornby Street dock, it runs from 7am to 8pm. For information contact **Granville Island Ferries** (☎ 684-7781) or **Aquabus Ferries** (☎ 689-5858).

INSURANCE

Cancellation Insurance

Your travel agent will usually offer you cancellation insurance when you buy your airline ticket or vacation package. This insurance allows you to be reimbursed for the ticket or package deal if your trip must be cancelled due to serious illness or death. Healthy people are unlikely to need this protection, which is therefore only of relative use.

Theft Insurance

Most residential insurance policies protect some of your goods from theft, even if the theft occurs in a foreign country. To make a claim, you must fill out a police report. It may not be necessary to take out further insurance, depending on the amount covered by your current home policy. As policies vary considerably, you are advised to check with your insurance company. European visitors should take out baggage insurance.

PRACTICAL INFORMATION

Life Insurance

Several airline companies offer a life insurance plan included in the price of the airplane ticket. However, many travellers already have this type of insurance and do not require additional coverage.

Health Insurance

This is the most useful kind of insurance for travellers, and should be purchased before your departure. Your insurance plan should be as complete as possible because health care costs add up quickly. When buying insurance, make sure it covers all types of medical costs, such as hospitalization, nursing services and doctor's fees. Make sure your limit is high enough, as these expenses can be costly. A repatriation clause is also vital in case the required care is not available on site. Furthermore, since you may have to pay immediately, check your policy to see what provisions it includes for such situations. To avoid any problems during your vacation, always keep proof of your insurance policy on your person.

HEALTH

General Information

Vaccinations are not necessary for people coming from Europe, the United States, Australia and New Zealand. On the other hand, it is strongly suggested, particularly for medium or long-term stays, that visitors take out health and accident insurance. There are different types so it is best to shop around. Bring along all medication, especially prescription medicine. Unless otherwise stated, the water is drinkable throughout British Columbia.

During the summer, always protect yourself against sunburn. It is often hard to feel your skin getting burned by the sun on windy days. Do not forget to bring sun screen!

Canadians from outside British Columbia should take note that in general your province's health care system will only reimburse you for the cost of any hospital fees or procedures at the going rate in your province. For this reason, it is a good idea to get additional private insurance. In case of accident or illness make sure to keep your receipts in order to be reimbursed by your province's health care system.

Emergencies

In case of emergency (police, fire department, ambulance), dial ☎ 911.

Emergency Phone Numbers

Police: ☎ 911, Vancouver ☎ 665-3535, Burnaby ☎ 294-7922
Firefighters: ☎ 911, Vancouver ☎ 665-6000, Burnaby ☎ 294-7190
Ambulance: ☎ 872-5151
Crime Stoppers: ☎ 669-8477
Emergency Hospital: ☎ 875-4995
To consult a family doctor, contact one of the many clinics, often open from 9am to 10pm, seven days a week (leaf through the yellow pages or call directory assistance at ☎ 411).
Dental Emergency: ☎ 736-3621 (College of Dental Surgeons). There are several dental clinics in the area (consult the yellow pages or call ☎ 411).
Poison Centre: ☎ 682-5050 or 682-2344
Crisis Centre (in case of emotional trauma): ☎ 872-3311
Veterinary Emergency Clinic (24 hours/day): ☎ 734-5104
Children's Emergency Help Line: dial 0 and ask for "Zenith 1234".
Help for Women: ☎ 872-8212
Legal Aid: ☎ 687-4680. 24-hour information service on laws in effect in British Columbia.
Roadside Assistance: ☎ 295-2222 (BCAA)

Hospitals

Children's Hospital: ☎ 875-2345
General Hospital: ☎ 875-4111
Burnaby Hospital: ☎ 434-4211
Lions Gate Hospital: ☎ 988-3131
St. Paul's Hospital: ☎ 682-2344
University Hospital: ☎ 822-7121

CLIMATE AND PACKING

The climate of Canada varies widely from one region to another. The Vancouver area benefits from a sort of micro-climate thanks to its geographic location between the Pacific Ocean and the mountains. Temperatures in Vancouver vary between 0°C and 15°C in the winter and much warmer in the summer.

If you plan on visiting other regions in Western Canada keep in mind factors like wind and altitude, which can cause a variety of weather conditions. Winters are cold and dry and temperatures can drop to -40°C, though the average is about -20°C. Summers are dry, with temperatures staying steady around 25°C in the south and lower in the mountains.

Average Daily High Temperatures °C/°F

January	5/41	July	23/74
February	7/44	August	23/74
March	10/50	September	18/65
April	14/58	October	14/58
May	18/65	November	96/48
June	21/69	December	6/43

Weather: Environment Canada, ☎ 664-9010

Winter

Vancouver has a particulary wet winter so don't forget your raincoat. In southern British Columbia the mercury rarely falls below 0°C. December to March remains the ideal season for winter-sports enthusiasts, who can enjoy many activities not far from the city (skiing, skating, etc.). Warm clothing is essential during this season (coat, scarf, hat, gloves, wool sweaters and boots) if you plan on visiting the mountains.

Spring and Fall

In Vancouver, spring and fall, and winter too for that matter, are hardly discernable. Spring is short (end of March to end of May), and conditions are generally rainy. Warmer temperatures encourage a beautiful blossoming of flowers. Fall is often cool and wet. A sweater, scarf, gloves, windbreaker and of course an umbrella are recommended for these low seasons.

Summer

Summer lasts from May to the end of August. Bring along t-shirts, lightweight shirts and pants, shorts and sunglasses; a sweater or light jacket is a good idea for evenings. If you plan on doing any hiking, remember that temperatures are cooler at higher altitudes.

 ACCOMMODATIONS

A wide choice of types of accommodation to fit every budget is available in Vancouver. Most places are very comfortable and offer a number of extra services. Prices vary according to the type of accommodation and the quality-to-price ratio is generally good, but remember to add the 7% G.S.T (federal Goods and Services Tax) and the provincial sales tax of 7%. The Goods and Services Tax is refundable for non-residents in certain cases (see p 59). A credit card will make reserving a room much easier, since in many cases payment for the first night is required.

PRACTICAL INFORMATION

Many hotels offer corporate discounts as well as discounts for automobile club (CAA, AAA) members. Be sure to ask about these special rates as they are generally very easy to obtain. Furthermore, check in the travel brochures given out at tourist offices as there are often coupons inside.

Hotels

Hotels rooms abound, and range from modest to luxurious. Most hotel rooms come equipped with private bathrooms. There are several internationally reputed hotels in Vancouver.

Inns

Often set up in beautiful historic houses, inns offer quality lodging. There are a lot of these establishments which are more charming and usually more picturesque than hotels. Many are decorated with beautiful period furniture. Breakfast is often included.

Bed and Breakfasts

Unlike hotels or inns, rooms in private homes are not always equipped with private bathrooms. There are many bed and breakfasts in Vancouver. Besides the obvious price advantage, the unique family atmosphere of these establishments is a plus. Credit cards are not always accepted in bed and breakfasts.

The following B&B associations can help you plan a stay in a bed and breakfast by providing addresses and occasionally making your reservations for you:

Beachside Bed & Breakfast Registry: 42008 Evergreen Ave., West Vancouver, V7H 1H1, ☎ 922-7773, ≠ 926-8073.

Old English Bed & Breakfast Registry: 1226 Silverwood, Cresc., North Vancouver, V7P 1J3, ☎ 986-5069, ≠ 986-8810

Best Canadian Bed & Breakfast Network: 1090 W. King Edward Ave., Vancouver, V6H 1Z4, ☎ 738-7207, ≠ 732-4998

Homestays

Regency International Cultural Exchange & Homestay Inc. *(2628 Granville St., Vancouver, V6H 3H8,* ☎ *222-1830,* ⇄ *222-8579)* can arrange homestays for short or long periods for families, business people or students.

Motels

There are many motels on the main access roads into the city. Though they tend to be cheaper, they often lack atmosphere. These are particularly useful when you are pressed for time.

University Residences

Due to certain restrictions, this can be a complicated alternative. Residences are generally only available during the summer (mid-May to mid-August); reservations must be made several months in advance, usually by paying the first night with a credit card.

This type of accommodation, however, is less costly than the "traditional" alternatives, and making the effort to reserve early can be worthwhile. Visitors with valid student cards can expect to pay approximately $25 plus tax. Bedding is included in the price, and there is usually a cafeteria in the building (meals are not included in the price).

 # RESTAURANTS

Excellent restaurants are easy to find in Vancouver. As an international crossroads of sorts, you can dine on just about anything in this city. A strong Asian presence and the proximity of the sea have a considerable effect of the types of cuisine offered. You'll also find restaurants in every budget range, from fast-food to fine dining.

Prices in this guide are for a meal for one person, excluding drinks and tip.

$ less than $10
$$ $10 to $20
$$$ $20 to $30
$$$$ more than $30

 ENTERTAINMENT

Bars and Discos

In most cases there is no cover charge, aside from the occasional mandatory coat-check. However, expect to pay a few dollars to get into discos on weekends. The legal drinking age is 19; if you're close to that age, expect to be asked for proof.

Wine, Beer and Alcohol

The legal drinking age is 19. Beer, wine and alcohol can only be purchased in liquor stores run by the provincial government.

 SHOPPING

In general, prices indicated on price tags for all goods do not include the sales tax (see below).

What to Buy

Salmon: you'll find this fish on sale, fresh from the sea, throughout the coastal areas of British Columbia.

Local crafts: paintings, sculptures, woodworking items, ceramics, copper-based enamels, weaving, etc.

Native Arts & Crafts: beautiful native sculptures made from different types of stone, wood and even animal bone are available, though they are generally quite expensive. Make sure the sculpture is authentic by asking for a certificate of authenticity issued by the Canadian government.

MONEY AND BANKING

Currency

The monetary unit is the dollar ($), which is divided into cents (¢). One dollar = 100 cents.

Bills come in 2-, 5-, 10-, 20-, 50-, 100-, 500- and 1000-dollar denominations, and coins come in 1- (pennies), 5- (nickels), 10- (dimes), 25-cent pieces(quarters), and in 1-dollar (loonies) and 2-dollar coins.

PRACTICAL INFORMATION

Exchange Rates

$1 = $0.69 US	$1 US = $1.45
$1 = 0.42 £	1£ = $2.40
$1 = $1.02 Aust	$1 Aust = $0.98
$1 = $1.16 NZ	$1 NZ = $0.86
$1 = 1.00 SF	1 SF = $1.00
$1 = 25.40 BF	10 BF = $0.39
$1 = 1.23 DM	1 DM = $0.81
$1 = 104 pesetas	100 pta = $0.96
$1 = 1213 lira	1000 lira = $0.82

Prices in this guide are in Canadian dollars.

Exchange

Most banks readily exchange American and European currencies but almost everyone of these will charge a **commission**. There are, however, exchange offices that do not charge commissions and keep longer hours. Just remember to **ask about fees** and **to compare rates**.

Custom House Currency Exchange: 375 Water St., ☎ 482-6000

International Securities Exchange: 1169 Robson St., ☎ 683-0604

Thomas Cook: 1016 W. Georgia St., ☎ 687-6111.

Money Services: Money Mart: ☎ 606-9555 or 930-5900 (24 hours/day)

Traveller's Cheques

Traveller's cheques are accepted in most large stores and hotels, however it is easier and to your advantage to change your cheques at an exchange office. For a better exchange rate buy your traveller's cheques in Canadian dollars before leaving.

Credit Cards

Most major credit cards are accepted at stores, restaurants and hotels. While the main advantage of credit cards is that they allow visitors to avoid carrying large sums of money, using a credit card also makes leaving a deposit for car rental much easier and some cards, gold cards for example, automatically insure you when you rent a car (check with your credit card company to see what coverage it provides). In addition, the exchange rate with a credit card is generally better. The most commonly accepted credit cards are Visa, MasterCard, and American Express.

Banks

Banks can be found almost everywhere and most offer the standard services to tourists. Visitors who choose to stay in Canada for a long period of time should note that **non-residents** cannot open bank accounts. If this is the case, the best way to have money readily available is to use traveller's cheques. Withdrawing money from foreign accounts is expensive. However, several automatic teller machines accept foreign bank cards, so that you can withdraw directly from your account. Money orders are another means of having money sent from abroad. No commission is charged but it takes time. People who have resident status, permanent or not (such as landed immigrants, students), can open a bank account. A passport and proof of resident status are required.

TAXES

The ticket price on items usually **does not include tax**. There are two taxes, the G.S.T. or federal Goods and Services Tax, of 7% and the P.S.T. or Provincial Sales Tax of 7%. They are cumulative and must be added to the price of most items and to restaurant and hotel bills. Some hotels charge an additional 8% provincial room tax.

There are some exceptions to this taxation system, such as books, which are only taxed with the G.S.T. and food (except for ready made meals), which is not taxed at all.

Tax Refunds for Non-Residents

Non-residents can obtain refunds for the G.S.T. paid on purchases. To obtain a refund, it is important to keep your receipts. Refunds up to $500 are obtained instantly from participating duty-free shops when leaving the country or by mailing a special filled-out form to Revenue Canada.

For information, call: ☎ 1-800-66-VISIT (1-800-668-4748) in Canada, or (902) 432-5608 from outside Canada.

TIPPING

In general, tipping applies to all table service: restaurants, bars and night-clubs (therefore no tipping in fast-food restaurants). Tips are also given in taxis and in hair salons.

PRACTICAL INFORMATION

The tip is usually about 15 % of the bill before taxes, but varies of course depending on the quality of service.

MAIL

Canada Post provides efficient (depending on who you talk to) mail service across the country. At press time, it cost 45¢ to send a letter elsewhere in Canada, 52¢ to the United States and 90¢ overseas. Stamps can be purchased at post offices and in many pharmacies and convenience stores.

Canada Post
General Information: ☎ 1-800-267-1177
Rates: ☎ 662-7222 (24 hours/day)
Postal Codes: ☎ 1-800-267-1133

TELECOMMUNICATIONS

The area code for telephone numbers in this guide is 604 unless otherwise indicated.

The area code for Vancouver and the lower mainland is ☎ 604. The area code for Vancouver Island, eastern, central and northern British Columbia is ☎ 250.

Long distance charges are cheaper than in Europe, but more expensive than in the U.S. Pay phones can be found everywhere, often in the entrances of larger department stores and in restaurants. They are easy to use and most accept credit cards. Local calls to the surrounding areas cost $0.25 for unlimited time. Have a lot quarters on hand if you are making a long distance call. It is less expensive to call from a private residence. 1-800 and 1-888 numbers are toll free.

BC Tel sells phone cards in various denominations for use in pay phones to place local and long distance calls.

You can have a phone installed for the length of your stay by calling **BC Tel** at ☎ 1-888-811-2323.

HOLIDAYS

The following is a list of public holidays in the province of British Columbia. Most administrative offices and banks are closed on these days.

January 1
Easter Monday and/or Good Friday
Victoria Day: the 3rd Monday in May
Canada Day: July 1st
Civic holiday (British Columbia Day): 1st Monday in August
Labour Day: 1st Monday in September
Thanksgiving: 2nd Monday in October
Remembrance Day: November 11 (only banks and federal government services are closed)
Christmas Day: December 25
Boxing Day: December 26

BUSINESS HOURS

Stores

Generally stores remain open the following hours:

Mon to Fri	10am to 6pm;
Thu and Fri	10am to 9pm;
Sat	9am or 10am to 5pm;
Sun	noon to 5pm

Well-stocked convenience stores that sell food are found throughout Vancouver and are open later, sometimes 24 hours a day.

Banks

Banks are open Monday to Friday from 10am to 4pm. Some are open on Thursdays and Fridays until 6pm or even 8pm and on weekends. Automatic teller machines are widely available and are open night and day.

Post Offices

Large post offices are open Monday to Friday from 9am to 5pm. There are also several smaller post offices located in shopping malls, convenience stores, and even pharmacies; these post offices are open much later than the larger ones.

SAFETY

By taking the normal precautions, there is no need to worry about your personal security. If trouble should arise, remember to dial ☎ **911**.

DISABLED TRAVELLERS

For information on wheelchair accessible attractions, banks, churches, parks, restaurants, stores and theatres get a copy of *Accessibility Awareness Vancouver Guide*. It is available from **The BC Coalition of People with Disabilities** *(204-456 W. Broadway, Vancouver, V5Y 1R3, ☎ 875-0188)*.

Public transportation is available from Handy Dart (see p 48).

CHILDREN

As in the rest of Canada, facilities exist in Vancouver that make travelling with children easy, whether it be for getting around or when enjoying the sights. Generally children under five travel for free, and those under 12 are eligible for fare reductions. The same applies for various leisure activities and shows. Find out before you purchase tickets. High chairs and children's menus are available in most restaurants, while a few of the larger stores provide a babysitting service while parents shop.

ADVICE FOR SMOKERS

As in the United States, cigarette smoking is considered taboo, and it is being prohibited in more and more public places. A Vancouver by-law prohibits smoking in all public places to which minors have access. This includes all restaurants and food courts in shopping malls, but does not include adult-only establishments which can designate smoking areas. The by-law applies only to the city of Vancouver proper, and therefore has limited scope, nevertheless check before lighting up!

Most public places (restaurants, cafés) have smoking and non-smoking sections. Cigarettes are sold in bars, grocery stores, newspaper and magazine shops.

TIME ZONE

Vancouver is on Pacific Standard Time. It is three hours behind Montreal and New York City, eight hours behind the United Kingdom and nine hours behind continental Europe. Daylight Savings Time (+ 1 hour) begins the first Sunday in April and ends on the last Sunday in October.

WEIGHTS AND MEASURES

Although the metric system has been in use in Canada for several years, some people continue to use the Imperial system in casual conversation. Here a some equivalents.

Weights
1 pound (lb) = 454 grams (g)
1 kilogram (kg) = 2.2 pounds (lbs)

Linear Measure
1 inch = 2.54 centimetres (cm)
1 foot (ft) = 30 centimetres (cm)
1 mile = 1.6 kilometres (km)
1 kilometre (km) = 0.63 miles
1 metre (m) = 39.37 inches

PRACTICAL INFORMATION

Land Measure
1 acre = 0.4 hectare
1 hectare = 2.471 acres

Volume Measure
1 U.S. gallon (gal) = 3.79 litres
1 U.S. gallon (gal) = 0.83 imperial gallon

Temperature
To convert °F into °C: subtract 32, divide by 9, multiply by 5
To convert °C into °F: multiply by 9, divide by 5, add 32.

ELECTRICITY

Voltage is 110 volts throughout Canada, the same as in the United States. Electricity plugs have two parallel, flat pins, and adaptors are available here.

ILLEGAL DRUGS

Recreational drugs are illegal and are not tolerated (even "soft" drugs). Anyone caught with drugs in their possession risks severe consequences.

LAUNDROMATS

Laundromats are found almost everywhere in urban areas. In most cases detergent is sold on site. Although change machines are sometimes provided, it is best to bring plenty of quarters (25¢) with you.

MOVIE THEATRES

There are no ushers and therefore no tips. Movie listings can be found in major newspapers. Movie tickets are considerably cheaper on Tuesdays.

MUSEUMS

Most museums charge admission. Reduced prices are available for people over 60, for children, and for students. Call the museum for further details.

NEWSPAPERS

The two principal newspapers in Vancouver are the *Vancouver Sun* and the *Vancouver Province*.

PHARMACIES

In addition to the smaller drug stores, there are large pharmacy chains which sell everything from chocolate to laundry detergent, as well as the more traditional items such as cough drops and headache medications. Shopper's Drug Mart is one of the largest chains of pharmacies in the city. Some of its branches are open 24 hours a day, for addresses see the "Shopping" chapter, p 194.

RELIGION

Almost all religions are represented.

RESTROOMS

Public restrooms can be found in most shopping centres. If you cannot find one, it usually is not a problem to use one in a bar or restaurant.

PRACTICAL INFORMATION

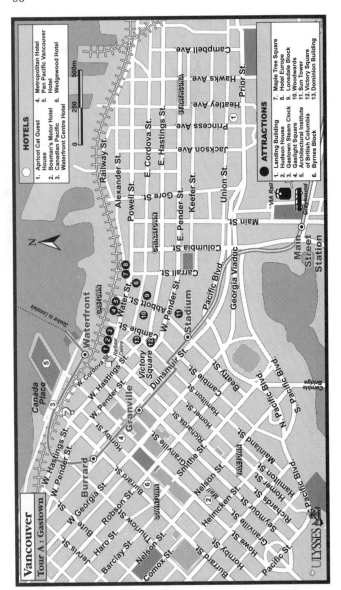

Vancouver
Tour A : Gastown

HOTELS
1. Apricot Cat Guest House
2. Bosman's Motor Hotel
3. Canadian Pacific Waterfront Centre Hotel
4. Metropolitan Hotel
5. Pan Pacific Vancouver Hotel
6. Wedgwood Hotel

ATTRACTIONS
1. Landing Building
2. Hudson House
3. Gaslight Square
4. Gastown Steam Clock
5. Architectural Institute of British Columbia
6. Byrnes Block
7. Maple Tree Square
8. Hotel Europe
9. Lonsdale Block
10. Woodwards
11. Sun Tower
12. Victory Square
13. Dominion Building

© ULYSSES

EXPLORING

T he following nine tours, each covering a different part of Vancouver, will help you fully enjoy the local sights. You can set out to explore the city's streets by taking Tour A: Gastown ★, Tour B: Chinatown and East Vancouver ★★, Tour C: Downtown ★★, Tour D: The West End ★, Tour E: Stanley Park ★★★, Tour F: Burrard Inlet ★★★, Tour G: False Creek ★, Tour H: South Vancouver and Shaughnessy ★★ or Tour I: The Peninsula ★★★.

Carrall Street serves as the dividing line between east and west in the centre of town (south of False Creek the border between east and west is Ontario Street). It also marks the border between Gastown, to the west, and Chinatown, to the east.

 TOUR A: GASTOWN ★

Just a few steps from downtown, Gastown is best discovered on foot. The area dates back to 1867, when John Deighton, known as Gassy Jack, opened a saloon for the employees of a neighbouring sawmill. Gastown was destroyed by fire in 1886. However, this catastrophe did not deter the city's pioneers, who rebuilt from the ashes and started anew the development of their city, which was incorporated several months later.

In the late 19th century, Gastown's economic development was driven by rail transport and the gold rush. The neighbourhood then became an important commercial distribution centre, but was later abandoned in favour of areas farther west. After a long period of decline, restoration was begun in the mid-1960s and continues to this day. Gastown's streets are now lined with little hotels, trendy cafés, restaurants, art galleries, souvenir shops and gaslit lanterns, and they make for a pleasant stroll.

Start off your tour at the corner of Water and West Cordova Streets, at the west edge of Gastown, which is accessible from the Waterfront station of the Skytrain.

The **Landing (1)** *(375 Water St.)*, with its brick and stone façade, was a commercial warehouse at the time of its construction in 1905; today it is a fine example of restoration. Since the late 1980s, it has housed offices, shops and restaurants.

Walk east along Water Street.

Like many other 19th-century North American buildings, **Hudson House (2)** *(321 Water St.)* has its back to the water and the natural setting. Erected in 1897 as a warehouse for the Hudson's Bay Company, it was renovated in 1977 in order to accentuate the pure lines of its red brick arches. The **Gastown Steam Clock (3)**, at the corner of Cambie Street, uses steam conducted through an underground network of pipes to whistle the hours. In clear weather, this spot affords a stunning view of the mountains north of the city.

Farther along Water Street, you will see the steep roofs of **Gaslight Square (4)** *(131 Water St.)*, a shopping centre laid out around a pretty inner court (Henriquez and Todd, 1975). Nearby are the offices of the **Architectural Institute of British Columbia ★ (5)** *(131 Water St., ste. 103; schedule and programme, ☎ 683-8588)*, which offers guided tours of Vancouver during the summertime.

The intersection of Water and Carrall Streets is one of the liveliest parts of Gastown. Long **Byrnes Block (6)** *(2 Water St.)*, on the southwest corner, was one of the first buildings to be erected after the terrible fire of 1886. It was built on the site of

Gassy Jack's saloon; a statue of the celebrated barkeep graces tiny **Maple Tree Square (7)**. The thick cornice on the brick building is typical of commercial buildings of the Victorian era. Rising in front is the former **Hotel Europe (8)** *(4 Powell St.)*, a triangular building erected in 1908 by a Canadian hotel-keeper of Italian descent.

Head south on Carrall Street, then turn right onto West Cordova.

Lonsdale Block (9) *(8-28 W. Cordova St.)*, built in 1889, is one of the most remarkable buildings on this street, which is undergoing a beautiful renaissance with the recent opening of several shops and, even more importantly, a number of cafés serving all different kinds of coffee made with freshly roasted beans. The coffee trend, which started in the American city of Seattle, less than 200 km from Vancouver, has really taken off along the old-fashioned streets of this neighbourhood. Long popular with artists, Gastown is now considered a tourist area, and unfortunately has become a bit pricey in places.

Turn left on Abbott Street.

At the corner of Hastings Street stands the former **Woodwards department store (10)** *(101 W. Hasting St.)*, founded in 1892 by Charles Woodward. It closed exactly 100 years later, following the death of the Woodward family patriarch, and was converted into 350 apartments during the summer of 1996. In the early 20th century, this part of Vancouver was the economic hub of the city. The shift of business to the west had a powerful impact on the area, both socially and economically. Today, part of Gastown is quite poor, and there are many vagrants here. Groups like the Downtown Eastside Residents Association defend the interests of those whose lives have been disrupted by the neighbourhood's recent overhaul, attempting to convince authorities to convert abandoned buildings into housing for the needy, so that people won't be forced to move to other parts of town.

EXPLORING

The south end of Abbott Street is dominated by the **Sun Tower ★ (11)** *(100 W. Pender St.)*, erected in 1911 for the *Vancouver World* newspaper. It later housed the offices of the local daily, *The Vancouver Sun*, after which it was named. At the time of its construction, the Sun Tower was the tallest building in all of the British Empire, although it only had 17 floors. Caryatids support its thick cornice, while its polygonal tower is topped by a copper-clad Beaux-Arts dome. This part of town is developing at breakneck speed; the new buildings east of the Sun Tower are part of a big project known as International Village, which should attract hundreds of new residents to the area.

Turn right on West Pender Street to reach Cambie Street and **Victory Square (12)**, in the centre of which stands **The Cenotaph**, a memorial to those who lost their lives in the two World Wars. It was sculpted by Thornton Sharp in 1924. The square acts like a pivot between the streets of Gastown and those of the modern business district. Facing onto the north side is the elegant **Dominion Building ★ (13)** *(207 W. Hastings St.)*, whose mansard roof is reminiscent of those found on Second Empire buildings along the boulevards of Paris.

Head north on Cambie Street to get back to where you started.

Turn left on West Cordova, where you'll find several triangular buildings, shaped in accordance with the streets, which intersect at different angles. Other buildings, with their series of oriel windows, are reminiscent of San Francisco.

★ TOUR B: CHINATOWN AND EAST VANCOUVER ★★

This tour starts at the intersection of Carall and East Pender. On East Pender Street, the scene changes radically. The colour and atmosphere of public markets, plus a strong Chinese presence, bring this street to life. The 1858 Gold Rush drew Chinese from San Francisco and Hong Kong; in 1878, railway construction brought thousands more Chinese to British Columbia. This community resisted many hard blows that might have ended its presence in the province. At the beginning of the 20th century, the Canadian government imposed a heavy tax on new Chinese immigrants, and then banned Chinese immigration altogether from 1923 to 1947. Today, the local

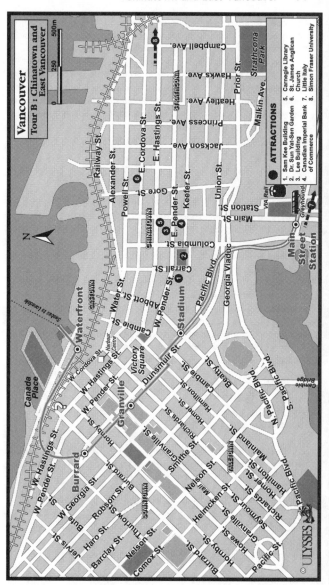

Vancouver
Tour B : Chinatown and
East Vancouver

ATTRACTIONS

1. Sam Kee Building
2. Dr. Sun Yat-Sen Garden
3. Lee Building
4. Canadian Imperial Bank
   of Commerce
5. Carnegie Library
6. St. James Anglican
   Church
7. Little Italy
8. Simon Fraser University

Chinese community is growing rapidly due to the massive influx of immigrants from Hong Kong, and Vancouver's Chinatown has become one of the largest in all of North America.

On your way into Chinatown, you'll see the strange little **Sam Kee Building (1)** *(8 W. Pender St.)*, which occupies a leftover piece of land barely two metres deep. Its interior space is augmented by the oriel windows overhanging the sidewalk and a basement that extends under the street. This area was once home to several famous brothels, as well as to a number of opium dens.

Take East Pender Street into the heart of Chinatown.

It is well worth stopping in at the **Dr. Sun Yat-Sen Garden ★ (2)** *(every day 10am to 7:30pm; 578 Carrall St., ☎ 689-7133)*, behind the traditional portal of the **Chinese Cultural Centre** at 50 East Pender Street. Built in 1986 by Chinese artists from Suzhou, this garden is the only example outside Asia of landscape architecture from the Ming Dynasty (1368-1644). The 1.2-hectare green space is surrounded by high walls which create a virtual oasis of peace in the middle of bustling Chinatown. At the beginning of the 20th century, the Canadian government imposed a tax on Chinese immigrants, then banned Chinese immigration altogether from 1923 to 1947. Today, the local Chinese community is growing rapidly, due to the massive influx of immigrants from Hong Kong, and Vancouver's Chinatown has become one of the largest in all of North America. It is worth noting that Dr. Sun Yat-Sen (1866-1925), considered the father of modern China, visited Vancouver in 1911 in order to raise money for his newly founded Kuomintang ("People's Party").

The architecture of the buildings along East Pender Street reflects the background of Vancouver's first Chinese immigrants, most of whom were Cantonese; take, for example, the deep, multi-story loggias on a number of the façades, such as that of the **Lee Building ★ (3)** *(129 E. Pender St.)*, built in 1907. To the left of this building is a passageway leading to a charming inner court surrounded by shops. During Chinese festivals, the loggias along East Pender Street are packed with onlookers, heightening the lively atmosphere.

Turn left on Main Street.

At the corner of East Pender Street stands a branch of the **CIBC (Canadian Imperial Bank of Commerce) (4)** *(501 Main St.)*, whose architecture was inspired by the English baroque style. Faced with terra cotta, this colossal edifice was designed by architect Victor Hosburgh and erected in 1915. Another example of the English baroque revival style is the former **Carnegie Library (5)** *(at the corner of Main and E. Hastings)*, now used as a community centre. This building owes its existence to American philanthropist Andrew Carnegie, who financed the construction of hundreds of neighbourhood libraries in the United States and Canada.

Turn right on East Cordova Street.

St. James Anglican Church ★ **(6)** *(303 E. Cordova)*, which stands at the corner of Gore Street, is one of the most unusual buildings to be erected in Canada between the two World Wars. A tall, massive structure made of exposed reinforced concrete, it was designed by British architect Adrian Gilbert Scott in 1935.

Head south on Gore Street to admire all the exotic products displayed along East Pender Street or enjoy a meal in one of the many Chinese restaurants there. If you wish to leave no stone unturned in your exploration of Vancouver's ethnic neighbourhoods, take Gore all the way to Keefer, turn right, then take a left on Main Street to reach Pacific Central Station (about a five-minute walk). Take the Skytrain toward Surrey, and get off at the next station (Broadway). If you're driving, head east on Georgia Street, turn onto Prior Street at the viaduct, then take a right on Commercial Drive.

When you get off the Skytrain, head north up Commercial Drive.

The next part of town you'll pass through is known as **Little Italy (7)**, but is also home to Vancouverites of Portuguese, Spanish, Jamaican and South American descent. In the early 20th century, the Commercial Drive area became the city's first suburb, and middle-class residents built small, single-family homes with wooden siding here. The first Chinese and Slavic immigrants moved into the neighbourhood during World War I, and another wave of immigrants, chiefly Italian, arrived at the end of World War II. North Americans will feel pleasantly out of

EXPLORING

their element in the congenial atmosphere of Little Italy's Italian cafés and restaurants. A few of these are listed in the "Restaurants" section (see p 154).

Some of Vancouver's most spectacular attractions are located outside the downtown area. To conclude your tour of East Vancouver, head to the city of Burnaby to visit **Simon Fraser University ★★ (8)** (SFU), located about a half-hour from the centre of Vancouver. If you don't have a car, take Bus #135 to the campus. Otherwise, drive east on East Hastings Street, take a right on Sperling Avenue, then a left on Curtis Street, which turns into Gagliardi Way.

Perched atop Mount Burnaby, SFU looks like a huge spaceship that just arrived here from another galaxy. The campus offers a panoramic view of downtown Vancouver, Burrard Inlet and the towering mountains to the north — a breathtaking sight in clear weather. The main buildings of bare concrete that form the nucleus of the university were designed in 1963 by the Canadian West's star architect Arthur Erickson and his associate Geoffrey Massey. Their architecture reflects the influence of Japanese temples, European cloisters, Mayan ruins and the Californian practice of leaving large parts of the exterior open. The grouping is laid out around a large courtyard. There is also a mall, half of which is sheltered by a glass and metal structure, so that students can enjoy pleasant temperatures winter and summer alike and find shelter from the region's frequent rainfalls.

 TOUR C: DOWNTOWN ★★

On May 23, 1887, Canadian Pacific's first transcontinental train, which set out from Montreal, arrived at the Vancouver terminus. The railway company, which had been granted an area roughly corresponding to present-day downtown Vancouver, began to develop its property. To say that it played a major role in the development of the city's business district would be an understatement. Canadian Pacific truly built this part of town, laying the streets and erecting some of the area's most important buildings. Downtown Vancouver has been developing continually since the 1960s — a sign of the city's great economic vitality, which can be attributed to Asian

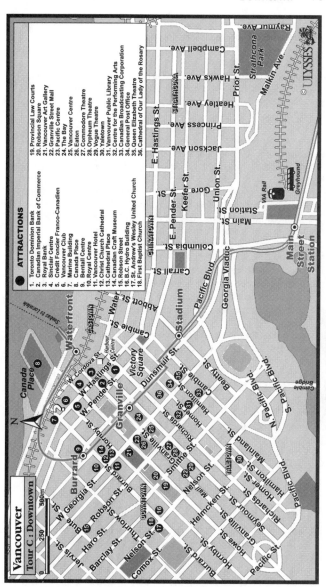

Vancouver
Tour C : Downtown

● **ATTRACTIONS**

1. Toronto Dominion Bank
2. Canadian Imperial Bank of Commerce
3. Royal Bank
4. Sinclair Centre
5. Crédit Foncier Franco-Canadien
6. Vancouver Club
7. Marine Building
8. Canada Place
9. Bentall Centre
10. Royal Centre
11. Vancouver Hotel
12. Christ Church Cathedral
13. Cathedral Place
14. Canadian Craft Museum
15. Robson Street
16. B.C. Hydro Building
17. St. Andrew's Wesley United Church
18. First Baptist Church
19. Provincial Law Courts
20. Robson Square
21. Vancouver Art Gallery
22. Granville Street Mall
23. Pacific Centre
24. The Bay
25. Vancouver Centre
26. Eaton
27. Commodore Theatre
28. Orpheum Theatre
29. Vogue Theatre
30. Yaletown
31. Vancouver Public Library
32. Centre for the Performing Arts
33. Canadian Broadcasting Corporation
34. General Post Office
35. Queen Elizabeth Theatre
36. Cathedral of Our Lady of the Rosary

EXPLORING

capital and the English Canadian population's shift westward, toward the mild climes of the Pacific coast.

This tour starts at the corner of West Hastings and Richards. Head west on West Hastings, toward the Marine Building, which will be directly in your line of vision. This tour can easily be combined with Tour A, which covers Gastown and ends nearby.

Located opposite Harbour Centre, the former regional headquarters of the **Toronto Dominion Bank (1)** *(580 W. Hastings St.)* exemplify the classical elegance of early 20th-century financial banking halls. The building has since been abandoned by the bank for one of the modern skyscrapers along Georgia Street. The former regional headquarters of the **Canadian Imperial Bank of Commerce (2)** *(640 W. Hastings St.)*, a veritable temple of finance, met the same fate and now house shops. This building, with its massive Ionic columns, was erected in 1906 according to a design by Darling and Pearson, whose credits include the Sun Life Building in Montreal. Opposite stands the massive **Royal Bank ★ (3)** *(675 W. Hastings St.)* building, designed by S. G. Davenport. The Italian Renaissance style banking hall is worth a look.

The **Sinclair Centre ★ (4)** *(701 W. Hastings St.)* is a group of government offices. It occupies a former post office, and its annexes are connected to one another by covered passageways lined with shops. The main building, dating from 1909, is considered to be one of the finest examples of the neo-baroque style in Canada. A little farther, at the corner of Hornby Street, is an austere edifice built in 1913 by the **Crédit Foncier Franco-Canadien (5)** *(850 W. Hastings St.)*, a financial institution jointly founded by French and Quebecois bankers. On the other side of the street, the **Vancouver Club (6)** *(915 W. Hasting St.)* is dwarfed by the skyscrapers on either side of it. Founded in 1914, it is a private club for businessmen, modelled after similar clubs in London.

The **Marine Building ★★ (7)** *(355 Burrard St.)*, which faces straight down West Hastings Street, is a fine example of the Art Deco style, characterized by vertical lines, staggered recesses, geometric ornamentation and the absence of a cornice at the top of the structure. Erected in 1929, the building lives up to its name, in part because it is lavishly

Sinclair Centre

decorated with nautical motifs, and also because its occupants are ship-owners and shipping companies. Its façade features terra cotta panels depicting the history of shipping and the discovery of the Pacific coast. The interior decor is even more inventive, however. The lights in the lobby are shaped like the prows of ships, and there is a stained glass window showing the sun setting over the ocean. The elevators will take you up to the mezzanine, which offers an interesting general view of the building.

Take Burrard Street toward the water to reach **Canada Place ★★ (8)** *(999 Canada Place)*, which occupies one of the piers along the harbour and looks like a giant sailboat ready to set out across the waves. This multi-purpose complex, which served as the Canadian pavilion at Expo '86, is home to the city's Convention Centre, the harbour station where ocean liners dock, the luxurious Pan Pacific Hotel and an Imax theatre. Take a walk on the "deck" and drink in the magnificent panoramic view of Burrard Inlet, the port and the snow-capped mountains.

Take Burrard Street back into the centre of town and continue southward to West Georgia Street.

On your way, you'll see the giant **Benthal Centre (9)** *(at the corner of Pender St.)*, made up of three towers designed by architect Frank Masson and erected between 1965 and 1975. You'll also see the **Royal Centre (10)** *(1055 W. Georgia St.)*, which includes the 38-story Royal Bank tower. These skyscrapers have to be "low" and squat in order to withstand the seismic activity in the Pacific Fire Crown.

The imposing **Hotel Vancouver ★ (11)** *(900 W. Georgia St.)*, a veritable monument to the Canadian railway companies that built it between 1928 and 1939, stands at the corner of West Georgia Street. For many years, its high copper roof served as the principal symbol of Vancouver abroad. Like all major Canadian cities, Vancouver had to have a Château-style hotel. Make sure to take a look at the gargoyles near the top and the bas-reliefs at the entrance, which depict an ocean liner and a moving locomotive.

The 23-story hotel dwarfs the tiny **Christ Church Cathedral (12)** *(690 Burrard St.)* facing it. This Gothic Revival Anglican cathedral was built in 1889, back when Vancouver was no more than a large village. Its skeleton, made of Douglas fir, is visible from inside. What is most interesting about the cathedral, however, is neither its size nor its ornamentation, but simply the fact that it has survived in this part of town, which is continually being rebuilt.

Flanking the cathedral to the east are the shops and offices of **Cathedral Place (13)** *(925 W. Georgia St.)*, built in 1991. Its pseudo-medieval gargoyles have not managed to make people forget about the Art Deco style Georgia Medical Building, which once occupied this site, and whose demolition in 1989 prompted a nation-wide outcry. Even with rock singer Bryan Adams' help, a major campaign to save the building proved futile. Cathedral Place is thus a building that is trying to gain acceptance; its pointed roof was modelled after that of the neighbouring hotel, and it is adorned with the stone nurses that once graced the Georgia Medical Building. The **Canadian Craft Museum (14)** *(Mon to Sat 10am to 5pm, Sun and holidays noon to 5pm, Thu to 9pm, Sep to May closed Tue; 639 Hornby St., ☎ 687-8266)* lies behind in a pretty little garden integrated into the project. This small, recently built spot houses a sampling of Canadian handicrafts production and a few decorative elements that were part of the Georgia Medical Building.

Head west on West Georgia Street.

Turn left on Thurlow Street and left again on **Robson Street ★ (15)**, which is lined with fashionable boutiques, elaborately decorated restaurants and West Coast-style cafés. People sit at tables outside, enjoying the fine weather and watching the motley crowd strolling by nonchalantly. This activity has become a veritable mania among coffee lovers; an American celebrity passing through Vancouver marvelled at the number of cafés on Robson Street, going so far as to declare that Vancouverites are addicted to coffee. If this is true, it hasn't changed the tempo of life here, which is known to be quite laid back. In the mid-20th century, a small German community settled around Robson Street, dubbing it Robsonstrasse, a nickname it bears to this day.

Return to Burrard Street, turn right and continue to Nelson Street.

EXPLORING

The former **B.C. Hydro Building ★ (16)** *(970 Burrard St.)*, at the corner of Nelson and Burrard, was once the head office of the province's hydroelectric company. In 1993, it was converted into a 242-unit co-op and renamed The Electra. Designed in 1955 by local architects Thompson, Berwick and Pratt, it is considered to be one of the most sophisticated skyscrapers of that era in all of North America. The ground floor is adorned with a mural and a mosaic in shades of grey, blue and green, executed by artist B.C. Binning. On the other side of the street stands **St. Andrew's Wesley United Church (17)**, which was built in 1931 and houses a window created by master glassworker Gabriel Loire of Chartres, France in 1969. The **First Baptist Church (18)** *(969 Burrard St.)*, located opposite, was erected in 1911.

Walk east on Nelson Street.

Turn left on Howe Street to view the **Provincial Law Courts ★ (19)** *(800 Smithe St.)* (1978), designed by talented Vancouver architect Arthur Erickson. The vast interior space, accented in glass and steal, is worth a visit. The courthouse and **Robson Square (20)** *(on the 800 block of Robson St.)*, by the same architect, form a lovely ensemble. Vancouver's luxuriant vegetation (sustained by abundant rainfall), unlike anything else in Canada, is put to maximum use here. Plants are draped along rough concrete walls and in between multiple little stepped ponds over which little water falls flow. Shops, restaurants and a skating rink welcome passers-by.

The **Vancouver Art Gallery ★ (21)** *($7.50; May 3 to Oct 9, Mon to Wed 10am to 6pm, Thu 10am to 9pm, Fri 10am to 6pm, Sat 10am to 5pm, Sun and holidays noon to 5pm, closed Mon and Tue during winter; 750 Hornby St., ☎ 662-4700)*, located north of Robson Square, occupies the former Provincial Law Courts. This big, neoclassical-style building was erected in 1908 according to a design by British architect Francis Mawson Rattenbury, whose other credits include the British Columbia Legislative Assembly and the Empress Hotel, both located in Victoria, on Vancouver Island. Later, Rattenbury returned to his native country and was assassinated by his wife's lover. The museum's collection includes a number of paintings by Emily Carr (1871-1945), a major Canadian painter whose primary subjects were the native peoples and landscapes of the West Coast.

Continue along Howe Street.

Turn right on West Georgia Street, then right again on the **Granville Street Mall ★ (22)**, the street of cinemas, theatres, nightclubs and retail stores. Its busy sidewalks are hopping 24 hours a day. The black skyscrapers at the corner of West Georgia belong to the **Pacific Centre (23)** *(on either side of Georgia St.)*, designed by architects Cesar Pelli and Victor Gruen (1969). A stainless steel sculpture by Greg Norris adorns the public square. Beneath the towers lie the beginnings of an underground city modelled after Montreal's, with 130 shops and restaurants. Opposite stands the Hudson's Bay Company department store (1913), better known as **The Bay (24)**. The company was founded in London in 1670, in order to carry out fur-trading operations in North America. In 1827, it became one of the first enterprises to set up shop in British Columbia. Across the street stand the **Vancouver Centre (25)** *(650 W. Georgia St.)*, which contains Scotia Bank's regional headquarters, and the **Vancouver Block** *(736 Granville St.)*, topped by an elegant clock. Finally, you can't miss the massive white **Eaton (26)** department store south of the Pacific Centre.

Stroll along the Granville Street Mall heading south towards Theatre Row. You'll pass the **Commodore Theatre (27)** *(870 Granville St.)* and the **Orpheum Theatre ★ (28)** *(884 Granville St., free tour upon reservation ☎ 665-3072)*. Behind the latter's narrow façade, barely eight metres wide, a long corridor opens onto a 2,800-seat Spanish-style Renaissance Revival theatre. Designed by Marcus Priteca, it was the largest and most luxurious movie theatre in Canada when it opened in 1927. After being meticulously restored in 1977, the Orpheum became the concert hall of the Vancouver Symphony Orchestra. Farther south, you'll see the vertical sign of the **Vogue Theatre (29)** *(918 Granville St.)*, erected in 1941. Today, popular musicals are presented in its Streamline Deco hall.

Turn left on Nelson and left again on Homer.

Located in the southeast of the downtown area, **Yaletown (30)** was an industrial area when the railways were still king. The growth of the trucking industry shifted business away from Yaletown's big warehouses, and the loading docks of Hamilton and Mainland streets have since been transformed into outdoor

EXPLORING

cafés and restaurants. A new group of tenants now occupies the old brick warehouses; designers, architects, film production companies and business people in general have brought this area back to life; trendy cafés and restaurants have followed suit.

At the corner of Robson Street is a curious building that is somewhat reminiscent of Rome's Coliseum. It is the **Vancouver Public Library ★★ (31)** *(free admission; year-round, Mon and Tue 10am to 9pm, Wed to Sat 10am to 6pm; Oct to Apr, Sun 1pm to 5pm, closed Sun in the summer; free tours can be arranged, ☎ 331-4041; 350 W. Georgia St., ☎ 331-3600)*. This brand-new building is the work of Montreal architect Moshe Safdie, known for his Habitat '67 in Montreal and the National Art Gallery in Ottawa. The project stirred lively reactions both from local people and from architecture critics. The design was chosen after finally being put to a referendum. The six-story atrium is positively grandiose. The **Ford Centre for the Performing Arts (32)**, completed in 1996, lies just opposite on Homer Street. Among other things, it contains an 1,800-seat theatre, whose orchestra seats, balcony and stage are depicted on the façade, north of the glass cone that serves as the entryway. These two buildings are sure evidence of Vancouver's thriving cultural scene.

Behind the library lies the long, low building of the **Canadian Broadcasting Corporation (33)**. The tubular structures on the façade are actually air ducts. The **General Post Office (34)** *(349 W. Georgia St.)*, north of the library, was built in 1953. Hidden behind it to the east is the **Queen Elizabeth Theatre (35)** *(630 Hamilton St.)*, designed chiefly by Montreal architects Ray Affleck and Fred Lebensold. It contains three theatres of different sizes. Its opening in 1959 foreshadowed the construction of similar complexes across North America, including New York's celebrated Lincoln Centre and Montreal's Place des Arts.

Take Homer Street north, then turn right on Dunsmuir Street.

To conclude your tour of downtown Vancouver, stop by the city's Catholic cathedral, the **Cathedral of Our Lady of the Rosary (36)** *(at the corner of Dunsmuir and Richards)*, erected in 1899. The rusticated stone facing and the wood and metal clock towers are reminiscent of parish churches built around the same time in Quebec.

 ## TOUR D: THE WEST END ★

Excluding Vancouver Island, farther west, the West End is the end of the line, the final destination of that quest for a better life that thousands of city-dwellers from Eastern Canada have been embarking upon for generations. People come here for the climate and the vegetation, no doubt, but also to escape the hustle and bustle and constraints of the older cities in the central and eastern parts of the country. It should come as no surprise, therefore, that despite all its concrete skyscrapers, the West End has a laid-back atmosphere, influenced both by the immensity of the Pacific and the wisdom of the Orient.

Because of this westward movement, and the fact that there is nowhere to go beyond here, the West End has the highest population per square kilometre of any area in Canada. Fortunately, nature is never far off, what with nearby Stanley Park (see p 86), stunning views of snow-capped mountains from the streets running north-south, or simply the sight of a cackling Canada goose strolling around a busy intersection.

This tour starts at the corner of Thurlow and Davie. Head west on the latter.

The population of the West End is a mixture of students and professionals, many of whom are getting rich, thanks to new technologies and the various new therapies now in fashion. The gay community is also well represented here. Residents of the local high-rises patronize the cafés, fast-food restaurants and grocery stores on Davie Street *(between Thurlow and Jervis)*. When you get to the corner of Nicola Street, take a look at **Rogers House (1)** *(1531 Davie St.)*, christened Gabriola by its owner when it was built in 1900. It was designed by one of the most prolific architects of well-heeled Vancouver society, Samuel Maclure. The house, with its numerous chimneys and circular gazebo, originally belonged to sugar magnate Benjamin Tingley Rogers, a native of New York. At the turn of the 20th century, the West End seemed destined to become an affluent suburb with large houses surrounded by gardens. One street was even given the pretentious name Blue Blood Alley. Things

EXPLORING

turned out otherwise, however, when the streetcar tracks were laid and a popular public beach on English Bay was opened in 1912. Gabriola is one of the only remaining houses of that era, and has since been converted into a restaurant.

Continue westward on Davie Street, then turn left on Bidwell Street to reach **Alexandra Park ★ (2)**, which forms a point south of Burnaby Street. It boasts a pretty wooden bandstand (1914) for outdoor concerts, as well as a marble fountain adorned with a brass plaque honouring Joe Fortes, who taught several generations of the city's children to swim. This luxuriant park also offers a splendid view of **English Bay Beach ★★ (3)** *(along the shore between Chilco and Bidwell Sts.)*, whose fine sands are crowded during the summer. The apartment high-rises behind it give beach-goers the illusion that they are lounging about at a seaside resort like Acapulco, when they are actually just a short distance from the heart of Vancouver. Few cities can boast beaches so close to their downtown core. Fleets of sailboats skim across the magnificent bay, which has recently been cleaned of pollutants and is bordered to the west by the verdant expanse of Stanley Park (see p 86).

After dipping your big toe in the Pacific Ocean (it's that close!), head back into town on Morton Avenue, where you'll see the **Ocean Towers (4)** *(1835 Morton Ave.)*, a cluster of jazzily shaped apartment buildings dating from 1957 (Rix Reinecke, architect). The previous year, Vancouver had modified the zoning regulation for the West End so that these high-rises could be built, provoking a frenzy among real-estate developers and leading to the construction of an interesting group of buildings that is as 1950s and "piña colada" as Miami Art Deco is 1930s and "dry martini". The Ocean Towers' neighbour to the west, the **Sylvia Hotel (5)** (see p 143) *(1154 Gilford St.)* is the oldest building on the beach. Its construction in 1912 sounded the death knell of the West End's country atmosphere. It is flanked by two post-modern buildings, **Eugenia Tower** and **Sylvia Tower**, topped in a very amusing fashion.

Head back east to Denman Street.

When they're not out surfing or sailboarding, the local beach bums often hang out around Denman and Davie Streets. The numerous restaurants in this area serve gargantuan brunches.

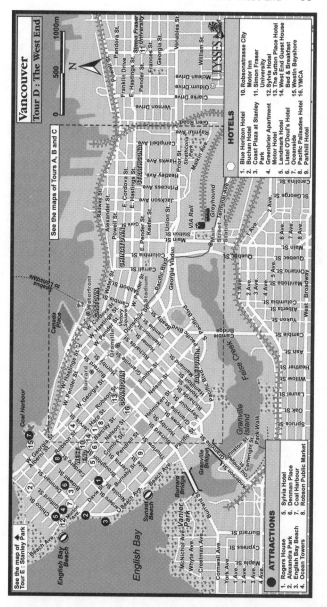

Vancouver

Tour D : The West End

See the map of
Tour E : Stanley Park

English Bay

Coal Harbour

HOTELS

1. Blue Horizon Hotel
2. Buchan Hotel
3. Coast Plaza at Stanley Park
4. Greenbrier Apartment Motor Hotel
5. Landmark Hotel
6. Listel O'Doul's Hotel
7. Oceanside
8. Pacific Palisades Hotel
9. Parkhill Hotel
10. Robsonstrasse City Motor Inn
11. Simon Fraser University
12. Sylvia Hotel
13. The Sutton Place Hotel
14. West End Guest House Bed & Breakfast
15. Westin Bayshore
16. YMCA

ATTRACTIONS

1. Rogers House
2. Alexandra Park
3. English Bay Beach
4. Ocean Towers
5. Sylvia Hotel
6. Denman Place
7. Coal Harbour
8. Robson Public Market

© ULYSSES

Continue north on Denman Street.

Denman Place (6) *(1733 Comox St.)*, at the corner of Comox Street, is a multi-functional complex made of bare concrete. Erected in 1968, it is home to the West End's largest shopping mall, complete with a supermarket, stores and movie theatres. The commercial area is topped by a 32-story tower containing apartments and a hotel.

Continue to the north end of Denman Street.

Take the path beside 1779 West Georgia Street to the waterfront and lovely **Coal Harbour ★ (7)**, which offers some outstanding views of Stanley Park and the mountains. You will also be greeted by a rather strange sight along the docks: a floating village of houseboats. The bay is full of yachts and sailboats, adding to the West End's seaside charm.

Go back to West Georgia, then take Bidwell south to Robson.

Head east on Robson Street, to the **Robson Public Market ★ (8)** *(1610 Robson, at the corner of Cardero)*, a bustling indoor market with a long glass roof. You'll find everything here from live crabs and fresh pasta to local handicrafts. You can also eat here, as dishes from all over the world are served on the top floor. A pleasure for both the palate and the eyes!

If your legs aren't too tired, take Robson Street east, back to downtown Vancouver and Thurlow Street. On the way, you'll pass countless shops, some with very creative window displays. You can also head downtown on bus #19, which runs along Georgia Street (two blocks north). During the ride, you will be treated to some spectacular views of the mountains of North and West Vancouver.

 TOUR E: STANLEY PARK ★ ★ ★

Lord Stanley, the same person for whom ice hockey's Stanley Cup was named, founded this park on a romantic impulse back in the 19th century, when he was Canada's Governor General (1888-1893). Stanley Park lies on an elevated peninsula stretching into the Georgia Strait, and encompasses

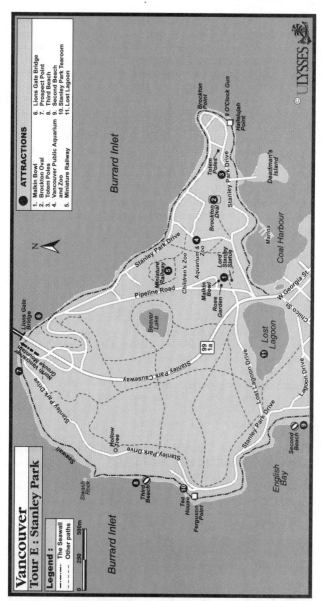

Vancouver
Tour E : Stanley Park

Legend :
- — — — The Seawall
- – – – Other paths

0   250   500m

ATTRACTIONS

1. Malkin Bowl
2. Brockton Oval
3. Totem Poles
4. Vancouver Public Aquarium and Zoo
5. Miniature Railway
6. Lions Gate Bridge
7. Prospect Point
8. Third Beach
9. Second Beach
10. Stanley Park Tearoom
11. Lost Lagoon

ULYSSES

Burrard Inlet

Coal Harbour

English Bay

Brockton Point

Hallelujah Point

Deadman's Island

Marina

9 O'Clock Gun

Stanley Park Drive

Totem Poles

Brockton Oval

Lord Stanley Statue

Aquarium & Zoo

Children's Zoo

Miniature Railway

Stanley Park Drive

Pipeline Road

Malkin Bowl

Rose Garden

Beaver Lake

Lions Gate Bridge

North Vancouver

Grouse Mountain

Stanley Park Drive

Prospect Point

Stanley Park Causeway

99 1a

Lost Lagoon

W Georgia St.

Chilco St.

Lost Lagoon Drive

Stanley Park Drive

Lagoon Drive

Second Beach

Stanley Park Drive

Tea House

Ferguson Point

Third Beach

Hollow Tree

Siwash Rock

Seawall

405 hectares of flowering gardens, dense woodlands and lookouts offering views of the sea and the mountains. Obviously Vancouver's many skyscrapers have not prevented the city from maintaining close ties with the nearby wilderness. Some species are held in captivity, but many others roam free — sometimes even venturing into the West End.

A ten-kilometre waterfront promenade known as the **Seawall** runs around the park, enabling pedestrians to drink in every bit of the stunning scenery here. The **Stanley Park Scenic Drive** is the equivalent of the Seawall for motorists. The best way to explore Stanley Park, however, is by bicycle. You can rent one from Stanely Park Rentals at the corner of West Georgia and Denman (☎ *688-5141*) (see "Cycling", p 123). Another way to discover some of the park's hidden treasures is to walk along one of the many footpaths crisscrossing the territory. There are numerous rest areas along the way.

From West Georgia Street, walk along Coal Harbour toward Brockton Point.

You'll be greeted by the sight of scores of gleaming yachts in the Vancouver marina, with the downtown skyline in the background. This is the most developed portion of the park, where you'll find the **Malkin Bowl (1)**, the **Brockton Oval (2)** and most importantly, the **Totem Poles ★ (3)**, reminders that there was a sizeable native population on the peninsula barely 150 years ago. The **9 O'Clock Gun** goes off every day at 9pm on Brockton Point (it is best not to be too close when it does). This shot used to alert fishermen that it was time to come in.

Continue walking along Burrard Inlet.

On the left is the entrance to the renowned **Vancouver Public Aquarium and Zoo ★★★ (4)** *(adults $12; Jul and Aug, every day 9:30am to 7pm; Sep to Jun, every day 10am to 5:30pm; ☎ 682-1118)*, which has the undeniable advantage of being located near the ocean. It displays representatives of the marine animal life of the West Coast and the Pacific as a whole, including magnificent killer whales, belugas, dolphins, seals and exotic fish. The zoo at the back is home to sea lions and polar bears, among other creatures. The nearby **Miniature Railway (5)** is a real hit with kids.

Polar Bear

Stanley Park harbours some lovely **flower gardens** ★, meticulously tended by a team of gardeners. Ask for Monsieur Gérard, a French gardener who has been working here for years; he'll show you "his" Stanley Park. Head back to the Seawall under **Lions Gate Bridge** ★★ **(6)**, an elegant suspension bridge built in 1938. It spans the First Narrows, linking the affluent suburb of West Vancouver to the centre of town. The two enormous lion's heads that greet you as you head onto the bridge were carved by artist Charles Marega. There is talk of increasing the bridge's capacity, either by building an upper roadway or by erecting a twin bridge to the east. **Prospect Point** ★★★ **(7)**, to the west, offers a general view of the bridge, whose steel pillars stand 135 metres high.

The **Seawall Promenade** runs along the edge the park, and after rounding a 45-degree bend offers a panoramic view of the Georgia Strait, with Cypress Park and Bowen Island visible in the distance on clear days. Next, it passes **Third Beach** ★ **(8)**, one of the most pleasant beaches in the region. The numerous cargo ships and ocean liners waiting to enter the port complement the setting.

We recommend stopping at the **Stanley Park Tearoom** ★ **(10)** (see Teahouse Restaurant, p 162), located between Third Beach and **Second Beach** ★ **(9)**. In the 1850s, the British government, fearing an American invasion (the U.S. border is less than 30 kilometres from Vancouver), considered building artillery batteries on this site. The risk of such a conflict had diminished by the early 20th century, so a charming tearoom was erected here instead. The Swiss-chalet-style building, surrounded by greenery, dates from 1911.

Complete the loop by taking the path to the **Lost Lagoon ★ (11)**, which was once part of Coal Harbour but was partially filled in during the construction of Lions Gate Bridge. It is now a bird sanctuary, where large numbers of barnacle geese, mallards and swans can be seen frolicking about.

 TOUR F: BURRARD INLET ★★★

Burrard Inlet is the long and very wide arm of the sea on which the Vancouver harbour — Canada's most important port for about twenty years now — is located. The Atlantic was once a favourite trading route, but the dramatic economic growth of the American West Coast (California, Oregon, Washington) and even more importantly, the Far East (Japan, Hong Kong, Taiwan, China, Singapore, Thailand, etc.), has crowned the Pacific lord and master of shipping.

Beyond the port lie the mountainside suburbs of North and West Vancouver, which offer some spectacular views of the city below. Along their steep, winding roads, visitors can admire some of the finest examples of modern residential architecture in North America. These luxurious houses, often constructed of posts and beams made of local wood, are usually surrounded by lofty British Columbian firs and a luxuriant blend of plants imported from Europe and Asia.

There are two ways to take this tour. The first is by foot: hop aboard the Seabus, the ferry that shuttles back and forth between downtown Vancouver and the north shore of Burrard Inlet, enjoy the open air and take in some exceptional views of both the city and the mountains. The other option is to drive across Lions Gate Bridge (see p 89), take Marine Drive east to Third Street and head south on Lonsdale Avenue. The following descriptions refer to the walking tour, unless otherwise indicated.

Start off your tour in front of the Neo-Classical Revival façade of the former **Canadian Pacific station ★ (1)** *(601 W. Cordova*

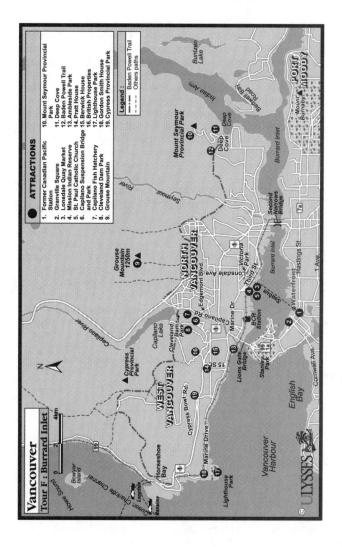

Vancouver
Tour F : Burrard Inlet

ATTRACTIONS

1. Former Canadian Pacific Station
2. Lonsdale Quay Market
3. Granville Square
4. Mission Indian Reserve
5. St. Paul Catholic Church
6. Capilano Suspension Bridge and Park
7. Capilano Fish Hatchery
8. Cleveland Dam Park
9. Grouse Mountain
10. Mount Seymour Provincial Park
11. Deep Cove
12. Baden Powell Trail
13. Ambleside Park
14. Pratt House
15. Berwick House
16. British Properties
17. Lighthouse Park
18. Gordon Smith House
19. Cypress Provincial Park

Legend :
— · — Baden Powell Trail
— — — Others paths

St.), which dates from 1912 and was designed by Montreal architects Barrott, Blackader and Webster. This station, Canadian Pacific's third in Vancouver, occupies a special place in the city's history, for before ships arriving from the west took over, trains arriving from the east fuelled the area's prosperous economy. In keeping with the times, the station no longer welcomes trains, but provides access to the Granville terminal of the Seabus. It also provides indirect access to the Waterfront terminal of the Skytrain (at the far end of Howe Street), but that's somewhat of a meagre consolation prize. Above the latter terminal is tiny **Portal Park** and its azaleas. **Granville Square (2)**, the skyscraper immediately to the west, is the only completed portion of a major real-estate development project (1971), which was to include the demolition of the train station.

Follow the signs for the Seabus. The crossing *($1.50)* takes barely a quarter of an hour, though you'll wish it were longer. The ferry lands at its northern terminal near the pleasant **Lonsdale Quay Market ★★ (3)**, built on a quay stretching out into Burrard Inlet. The cafés surrounding the market offer an unimpeded view of Vancouver and the mountains, as well as all the activity at the nearby port, for the colourful tugboat dock flanks the market to the east. Built in 1986, Lonsdale Quay Market was the brainchild of architects Hotson and Bakker, who wanted to satisfy every basic human need here: food (ground floor), clothing (second floor) and lodging (upper floors, see p 148). From here, Vancouver really looks like a Manhattan in the making.

The market is the main urban attraction in North Vancouver, a suburb of 68,000 people sandwiched between Burrard Inlet and mountains over 1,500 metres high. The urbanization of the north shore of the inlet began in the second half of the 19th century, when a number of businessmen from New Westminster decided to make capital of the firs, hemlock spruce and red cedars in the surrounding forest. It was Maine (U.S.A.) native Sewell Prescott Moody, however, who made British Columbia's wood known around the world. Ferry service between Gastown (see p 67) and "his" town, Moodyville, was introduced in 1866. At the beginning of the 20th century, most of the property in North and West Vancouver was transferred to British interests, who began developing the areas as residential suburbs.

North of the market, you can enjoy a pleasant stroll along Lonsdale Avenue. The old banks and public buildings bear witness to the prosperous past of the wood industry. Keep walking until you reach Victoria Park, then head west on Sixth Street to return to Burrard Inlet. On either side of the market, the east shore is scattered with tiny native reserves, some barely two blocks across. One of these is the **Mission Indian Reserve (4)**, centred around Mission Road, which leads to West Esplanade. There you will find the **St. Paul Catholic Church (5)**, erected between 1884 and 1909 by Oblate missionaries from Quebec. The interior is decorated with stained-glass windows and polychrome statues.

If you are travelling by car, return to Marine Drive heading west and go up Capilano Road until you reach the **Capilano Suspension Bridge and Park (6)** *(9$; May to Oct 8am to 9pm; Nov to Apr 9am to 5pm; 3735 Capilano Rd., ☎ 985-7474)*. If you are on foot at Lonsdale Quay Market, take bus number 236 to Edgmont Boulevard. Paths lead to this metal-cabled bridge, suspended 70 metres above the Capilano River, which replaced the original bridge of rope and wood built in 1899. The presence of indigenous peoples is more evident in British Columbian society than in any other Canadian province. A number of them gather in this park each summer to carve totem poles.

Three kilometres to the north is the **Capilano Fish Hatchery ★ (7)** *(free entry; 4500 Capilano Park Rd., ☎ 666-1790)* the first pisciculture farm in British Columbia. This well-laid-out spot provides visitors with an introduction to the life cycle of the salmon. In the summer, Pacific salmon wear themselves out as they make their way up the Capilano River to reach the reproduction centre, making for an exceptional spectacle for visitors.

The upper part of Upper Capilano Road was renamed Nancy Greene Way, after the Canadian skier who won the gold medal for the giant slalom at the 1968 Olympics in Grenoble, France. On the left, a road leads to **Cleveland Dam Park ★★ (8)**, on the shores of Lake Capilano. The construction in 1954 of the impressive 100-metre-high dam at the centre of the park lead to the creation of the lake, Vancouver's main source of drinking water. Spectacular views of the neighbouring mountains, surround the park.

EXPLORING

At the north end of Nancy Greene Way, there is a **cable car** *($16; summer every day 9am to 10pm, Sat and Sun 8am to 10pm;* ☎ *984-0661)* that carries passengers to the top of **Grouse Mountain ★★★ (9)** , where, at an altitude of 1,250 m, skiers and hikers can contemplate the entire Vancouver area, as well as Washington State (in clear weather) to the south. The view is particularly beautiful at the end of the day. Wilderness trails lead out from the various viewing areas. During summer, Grouse Mountain is also a popular spot for hang-gliding.

Among the other sights in North Vancouver that are accessible by car and worth mentioning, is **Mount Seymour Provincial Park ★★ (10)** *(Mount Seymour Parkway)* where skiing is possible both day and night. In addition, there are a number of cross-country trails, which become hiking paths in the summer. **Deep Cove (11)**, at the eastern edge of North Vancouver, on the shore of Indian Arm, is a fine spot for canoeing and kayaking. Close to the village is the head of the **Baden Powell Trail ★★ (12)**, which runs through the wilderness all the way to Horseshoe Bay, 42 kilometres to the west.

The Burrard Inlet walking tour ends at Grouse Mountain.

To return to Vancouver, get on the bus again, then take the Seabus back the other way. Motorists can continue exploring the area by heading to **West Vancouver ★★** *(go back down Upper Capilano Rd., then turn right on Marine Dr.)*, a fashionable residential suburb located on a mountainside. A number of talented architects have helped enrich the city's modern heritage.

Marine Drive leads past two large shopping centres. **Ambleside Park ★ (13)**, located to the west of these, is worth a stop, as it offers some lovely views of Stanley Park and Lions Gate Bridge. Near the water, landscape architect Don Vaughan created the **Waterside Fountain** out of cubes of granite in 1989. West of the park, an attractive promenade leads along the water to 24th Street.

Turn right on 15th Street, then right again on Lawson Avenue, where you'll find **Pratt House (14)** *(1460 Lawson Ave.; not open to the public)*, designed by architect C.E. Pratt in 1948 for his own use. Pratt was a great promoter of this style of wooden house, which is open on the outside and blends into the natural environment. Although designed to withstand earthquakes and resist rotting due to the heavy rainfall here (wide-edged roofs, cedar construction), these houses might appear fragile to Europeans more accustomed to stone and brick buildings.

The nearby **Berwick House (15)** *(1650 Mathers Ave.; not open to the public)*, designed by the architect of the same name, dates back to 1939, and was thus a forerunner of this type of construction. Since the 1930s, Canadian architects working on the West Coast have been greatly influenced both by the Californian buildings of the Greene brothers and Richard Neutra, and by much older Japanese designs dating from the time of the *shoguns*.

Head north on 15th Street, which becomes Cross Creek Road and then Eyremount Drive.

Next, you'll reach **British Properties ★ (16)** *(on either side of the road starting at Highland Dr.)*, where untouched woodlands and suburbia overlap. British Pacific Properties Limited, owned by London's famous Guinness family, known for their stout, began developing this mountainous area in 1932. The overall design was the work of the Olmsted Brothers, the worthy successors of Frederick Law Olmsted, whose credits include Montreal's Mount Royal Park and New York's Central Park.

Return to Marine Drive.

Turn right on Marine Drive and continue to **Lighthouse Park ★ (17)** *(entrance on Beacon Lane)*, located on a point that stretches out into the Strait of Georgia and has a lighthouse on its southern tip. Strolling around this peaceful place truly evokes a feeling of infinite space. The nearby **Gordon Smith House (18)** *(The Byway via Howe Sound Lane; not open to the public)* is a West Coast version of the glass houses of Mies van der Rohe and Philip Jonson. Designed by Erickson and Massey, it was built in 1965. Arthur Erickson, who is also mentioned in the previous tours, designed the Canadian embassy in Washington as well.

Like the TransCanada Highway, Marine Drive ends at the port of the village of **Horseshoe Bay ★**, where the terminal for the

EXPLORING

ferry to Vancouver Island is located. To return to Vancouver, head east on the TransCanada Highway, then follow the signs for Lions Gate Bridge. On the way, there is an exit for **Cypress Bowl Road**, a scenic road whose steep hills are ill-suited to cars with weak engines. It leads to **Cypress Park ★★★ (19)** and Cypress Bowl itself, a mountain where skiers can enjoy a 900-metre vertical drop and breathtaking views of the Strait of Georgia.

 TOUR G: FALSE CREEK ★

False Creek is located south of downtown Vancouver and, like Burrard Inlet, stretches far inland. The presence of both water and a railroad induced a large number of sawmills to set up shop in this area in the early 20th century. These mills gradually filled a portion of False Creek, leaving only a narrow channel to provide them with water, which is necessary for sawing. Over the years, two thirds of False Creek, as explorer George Vancouver had known it in 1790, disappeared under asphalt. In 1974, when the local sawmills shut down en masse, people began moving into new housing developments the likes of which were becoming more and more popular around the world by that time. Then, in 1986, False Creek hosted Expo '86, attracting several million visitors here in the space of a few months.

Get off at the Skytrain's Main Street Station, located opposite the long Beaux-Arts façade of **Pacific Central Station (1)** *(1150 Station St.)*. Determined not to be outdone, Canadian National (formerly the Canadian Northern Pacific Railway Company) copied Canadian Pacific by building a second transcontinental railway, which ran parallel to the first and ended at this station, erected in 1919 on the embankment of False Creek. Today, it welcomes Canadian VIA trains and American Amtrak trains, as well as various private trains which use the tracks running through the Rockies for scenic tours.

Head over to **Science World ★ (2)** *($10.50 or $13.50 with movie; 1455 Quebec St., ☎ 443-7440)*, the big silver ball at the end of False Creek. Architect Bruno Freschi designed this 14-story building as a welcome centre for visitors to Expo '86. It was the only pavilion built to remain in place after the big event. The sphere representing the Earth has supplanted the

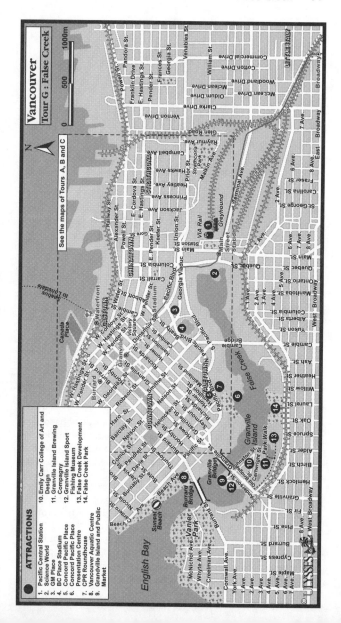

Vancouver
Tour G : False Creek

See the maps of Tours A, B and C

ATTRACTIONS

1. Pacific Central Station
2. Science World
3. GM Place
4. BC Place Stadium
5. Concord Pacific Place
6. Concord Pacific Place Presentation Centre
7. CPR Roundhouse
8. Vancouver Aquatic Centre
9. Granville Island and Public Market
10. Emily Carr College of Art and Design
11. Granville Island Brewing Compagny
12. Granville Island Sport Fishing Museum
13. False Creek Development
14. False Creek Park

ULYSSES

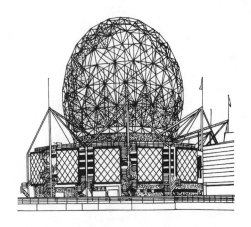

Science World

tower as the quintessential symbol of these fairs since Expo
'67 in Montreal. Vancouver's sphere contains an Omnimax
theatre, which presents films on a giant, dome-shaped screen.
The rest of the building is now occupied by a museum that
explores the secrets of science from all different angles.

*Walk alongside False Creek to Pacific Boulevard South before
plunging into the void beneath Cambie Bridge.*

During the summer of 1986, the vast stretch of unused land
along the north shore of False Creek was occupied by dozens
of showy pavilions with visitors crowding around them. Visible
on the other side of an access road, **GM Place (3)** *(Pacific Blvd.
at the corner of Abbott,☎ 899-7400)* is a 20,000-seat
amphitheatre which was completed in 1995 and now hosts the
home games of the local hockey and basketball teams, the
Vancouver Canucks and Grizzlies respectively. Its big brother,
BC Place Stadium (98) *(777 Pacific Blvd. N., ☎ 669-2300,
661-7373 or 661-2122, ⇌ 661-3412)* stands to the south. Its
60,000 seats are highly coveted by fans of Canadian football,
who come here to cheer on the B.C. Lions. Big trade fairs and
rock concerts are also held in the stadium.

Development of the grounds of Expo '86 has made good progress due to the city's thriving economy and thanks to the capital that flowed out of Hong Kong on the eve of the British colony's return to communist China in 1997. There are plans to build high-rises containing thousands of apartments and flanked by gardens similar to those in the West End. The first phase of the project known as **Concord Pacific Place (5)**, named after a major Hong Kong real-estate developer, was completed in 1994. The high-rises, whose architecture resembles that of Battery Park City in New York, line Pacific Boulevard between Homer and Cambie Streets. A model of the entire project is on display at the **Concord Pacific Place Presentation Centre (6)**, on the waterfront.

The beautifully restored **CPR Roundhouse ★ (7)** *(at the corner of Davie St. and Pacific Blvd.)*, located opposite, is all that remains of the Canadian Pacific marshalling yard once located on this site. Erected in 1888, it was used for the servicing and repair of locomotives. The mammoth iron machines were pivoted around on single track so that they could be repaired behind one of the 10 doors of this "garage". Granville Island is visible across the water, as are the new residential areas along False Creek.

Follow Pacific Boulevard under Granville Bridge, then turn left on Hornby Street and right on Beach Avenue. This will lead you to the **Vancouver Aquatic Centre (8)** *(☎ 665-4324)*, a large indoor public pool and gym located on the other side of the Burrard Street Bridge.

The False Creek ferry docks are located behind this centre. Get on board the boat for **Granville Island and its public market ★★ (9)**. You'll notice the vaguely Art Deco pillars of the Burrard Street Bridge (1930). In 1977, this artificial island, created in 1914 and once used for industrial purposes, saw its warehouses and factories transformed into a major recreational and commercial centre. The area has since come to life thanks to a revitalization project. A public market, many shops and all sorts of restaurants, plus theatres and artists' studios, are all part of Granville Island. You will also find a community centre and the **Emily Carr College of Art and Design (10)**, which was enlarged considerably in 1996 and presents exhibitions of work by students and various artists from British Columbia. Not to be missed on the island is the micro-brewery tour offered by the

Granville Island Brewing Company (11) *(summer, Mon to Thu 9:30am to 7pm, Fri and Sat to 8pm; guided tours $6, summer every day noon to 5pm on the hour; winter every day, call ahead for store and tour schedules; 1441 Cartwright St., ☎ 687-BREW)*. The newly renovated facilities, opened in late May 1997 include a specialty beer and wine store, a tasting-room and a brewhouse. Avoid taking your car onto the island; traffic jams are common, and parking is hard to find. To reach the island without following the False Creek tour take bus number 50 heading south from Howe Street downtown.

On the island, take Anderson Street south alongside Granville Bridge, then turn left on Park Walk.

Granville Island Sport Fishing Museum (12) *(1502 Duranleau, Granville Island, ☎ 683-1939)*. This museum boasts an international collection of artifacts — some very old — all related to sport fishing in British Columbia. It is situated in the heart of Granville Island, a stone's throw from the large covered market. The exhibits dedicated to fly-fishing are the most impressive. Here you will enter a fascinating world, one full of rituals where ecology and entomology is a prerequisite to knowledge of successful fly-fishing. Once you have caught the "bug", after visiting this lovely museum, you will have the urge to equip yourselves and head for the great outdoors. The museum's information centre offers a complete list of outfitters, lodges, clubs and the best fishing spots in British Columbia.

You will now enter the **False Creek Development ★ (13)** , a residential area begun in 1974 and built in stages by private developers on formerly insalubrious government land. It is pleasant to wander about on the pedestrian walkways around **False Creek Park (14)** and look at the carefully designed groups of houses.

TOUR H: SOUTH VANCOUVER AND SHAUGHNESSY ★★

This tour covers two separate neighbourhoods located south of False Creek, the City Hall area and the Shaughnessy Heights area.

Vancouver

Tour H : Shaughnessy

0   500   1000m

© ULYSSES

HOTELS
1. Pillow Porridge Guest House
2. Plaza 500 Hotel
3. William House

ATTRACTIONS
1. City Hall
2. Vancouver General Hospital
3. Walter C. Nichol House
4. McRae House
5. Van Dusen Botanical Gardens
6. Queen Elizabeth Park

In the 1930s, the municipal government planned to make the first area of this tour Vancouver's new downtown core, in an effort to shift the city centre. This involved building a new city hall near Broadway. It is true that when you look at a map, you realize that Vancouver's business section is located at the northern edge of town, on a peninsula accessible mainly by bridges. Practical as it was, however, the project was a bitter failure, as illustrated by the solitary tower of City Hall, rising up amidst scores of cottage-style houses.

The second area, Shaughnessy Heights, is an affluent residential enclave, which Canadian Pacific began building in 1907. It succeeded the West End as a refuge for well-heeled Vancouverites. The area was named after Thomas G. Shaughnessy, who was president of C.P. at the time and lived in the house of the same name in Montreal, which is now part of the Canadian Centre for Architecture. A number of local streets, furthermore, were named after the eminent families of Montreal's Golden Square Mile, like the Hosmers, the Oslers and the Anguses.

The tour starts at the corner of Cambie and Broadway.

Head south on Cambie Street to **City Hall (1)** *(453 W. 12th Ave.)*, a massive, austere-looking tower topped by public clocks and featuring both classical and Art Deco elements (1935).

Head west on 12th Avenue.

Next, you will pass **Vancouver General Hospital (2)** *(855 W. 12th Ave.)*, one of the largest hospitals in North America. Several of its buildings were erected in the Streamline Deco style between 1944 and 1950. Unlike the geometric, vertical Art Deco style, the Streamline Deco or "steamship" style features rounded, horizontal lines, which symbolize speed and modernism.

Turn left on Oak Street, then right on 16th Ave..

Take Tecumseh Avenue into Shaughnessy Heights and walk around The Crescent to get a taste of the opulence of the houses in this area. Of all the houses, the most elegant is definitely **Walter C. Nichol House ★ (3)** *(1402 The Crescent; not open to the public)*, a masterpiece by Maclure and Fox,

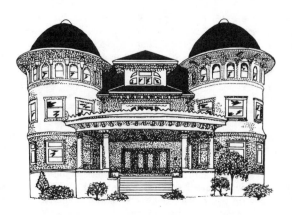

One of Shaughnessy's Stately Residences

built in 1912 for the former Lieutenant Governor of British Columbia. The half-timbering and mullioned windows typical of English farms and manors are clear reminders of the British roots that characterize this province, despite its great distance from the mother country. Furthermore, as the climate is similar to that of England, these houses boast front gardens as lovely as those found on the outskirts of London.

Steal along McRae Avenue, where you'll find the largest home in Shaughnessy Heights, **McRae House ★ (4)** *(1489 McRae Ave.)*, also known as Hycroft. Built in 1909 for General Alexander McRae, it was designed by Thomas Hooper. The long façade has a projecting portico in the Beaux Arts spirit. The interior, decorated by Charles Marega, who sculpted the lions for Lions Gate Bridge, boldly combines Italian rococo with English neoclassicism. Like many other mansions across Canada, McRae House was abandoned by its owners and liveried servants after the stock market crash of 1929. Since 1961, it has been occupied by the University Women's Club.

Go back and complete the loop of The Crescent, then take Osler Avenue southward out of Shaughnessy Heights.

Turn left on 33rd Avenue, then right on Oak Street, where you'll find the entrance to the **Van Dusen Botanical**

EXPLORING

Gardens ★★ (5) *(summer $5.50, winter $2.75; every day, summer 10am to nightfall, call for exact schedule; Apr and Sep 10am to 6pm; Oct to Mar 10am to 4pm; free guided tours every day, 1pm, 2pm and 3pm; 5251 Oak St., ☎ 878-9274).* Since Vancouver is so blessed by Mother Nature, a number of lovely gardens have been planted in the area, including this one, which boasts plant species from all over the world. When the rhododendrons are in bloom (late May), the garden deserves another star. At the far end is a housing co-op that blends in so perfectly with the greenery that it looks like a gigantic ornamental sculpture (McCarter, Nairne and Associates, 1976).

Farther east on 33rd Avenue is another magnificent green space, **Queen Elizabeth Park (6) ★★** *(corner of 33rd Ave. and Cambie St.),* laid out around the **Bloedel Floral Conservatory** *($3.25; Apr to Sep, Mon to Fri 9am to 8pm, Sat and Sun 10am to 9pm; Oct to Mar, every day 10am to 5pm; at the top of Queen Elizabeth Park, ☎ 257-8570).* The latter, shaped like an overturned glass saucer, houses exotic plants and birds. The Bloedel company, which sponsored the conservatory, is the principal lumber company in British Columbia. This park's rhododendron bushes also merit a visit in springtime. Finally, the outdoor gardens offer a spectacular view of the city, English Bay and the surrounding mountains.

The walking tour ends here. Catch bus #15 on Cambie Street to go back downtown.

One of the other attractions in South Vancouver that visitors with cars can visit is the second biggest **Buddhist temple (7)** in North America *(every day 10am to 5pm; 9160 Steveston Highway, Richmond, ☎ 274-2822).* To get there, take Oak Street southward toward Highway 99, which leads to the ferry for Victoria, and get off at the Steveston Highway West exit. Located between the third and fourth streets on your left, this place of worship has free entry.

Get back on the Steveston Highway heading west, turn left on 4th Avenue, and continue to the end of this avenue. The **Georgia Cannery ★ (8)** *(3$; July and Aug, every day 10am to 5pm; May, Jun and Sep, Thu to Mon 10am to 5pm; guided tours every hour; 12138 4th Ave., Richmond, ☎ 664-9009),* restored by Parks Canada, retraces the history of the fishing industry in Steveston. This historical spot explains the steps

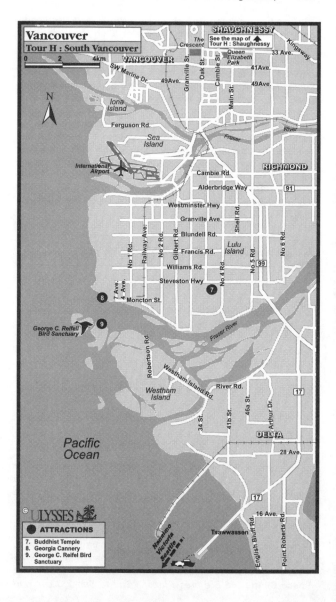

involved in conserving fish, especially salmon, and also shows how herring is transformed into pet food and oil. Very interesting. Leaving this establishment, stay along the seashore by way of the wooden walkway near the fishing boats. Fishing remains an important economic activity in this region. A commercial area with restaurants and shops invites you to relax. The day's catch is served in the restaurants.

Turn back along the Steveston Highway, this time heading east, and take Route 99 toward the ferry pier for Victoria; take the Ladner exit after the tunnel. Go along this road and follow the signs to the **George C. Reifel Bird Sanctuary ★★ (9)** *(adults $3.25; every day 9am to 4pm, 5191 Robertson Rd., Delta, ☎ 946-6980)*. Each year more than 350 species of birds visit this magical spot in the marshlands at the mouth of the Fraser River.

TOUR I: THE PENINSULA ★★★

The culture of the Pacific as well as the history and traditions of the native peoples are omnipresent throughout this tour which follows the shore of the vast peninsula that is home to the majority of Vancouver's residents. Posh residential neighbourhoods, numerous museums, a university campus and several sand and quartz beaches from which Vancouver Island is visible on a clear day all make up this tour. This is a driving tour as it extends over 15 kilometres. The first four attractions are accessible aboard bus # 22 from downtown or by taking bus # 4 directly to the campus of the University of British Columbia.

Exit the downtown area by the Burrard Street Bridge.

Keep right, and immediately after going down the roadway leading off the bridge, take a right on Chestnut Street to get to **Vanier Park (1)**, which is home to three museums. The **Vancouver Museum ★★** *($5; Jul and Aug, every day 10am to 5pm; Sep to June closed Mon; 1100 Chestnut St., in Vanier Park, ☎ 736-4431)* forms its centrepiece. This museum, whose dome resembles the head-dress worn by Coast Salish Indians, presents exhibitions on the history of the different peoples who have inhabited the region. At the same spot is the **Pacific Space Centre** *($6.50; presentations Tue to Sun 2:30pm and*

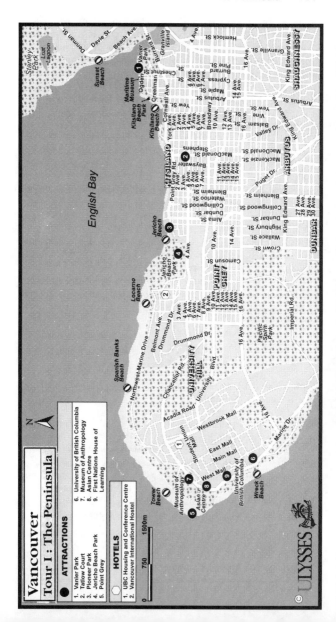

Vancouver
Tour I : The Peninsula

ATTRACTIONS

1. Vanier Park
2. Tatlow Court
3. Pioneer Park
4. Jericho Beach Park
5. Point Grey
6. University of British Columbia
7. Museum of Anthropology
8. Asian Centre
9. First Nations House of Learning

HOTELS

1. UBC Housing and Conference Centre
2. Vancouver International Hostel

8pm, extra shows Sat and Sun 1pm and 4pm; Ms. Dawn Charles, ☎ *738-7827),* which houses the H.R. MacMillan Planetarium and relates the creation of our universe. It has a telescope through which you can admire the stars. The **Maritime Museum** *($6; May to Oct, every day 10am to 5pm; Nov to Apr closed Mon; 1905 Ogden Ave.,* ☎ *257-8300)* completes the trio of institutions in Vanier Park. Being a major seaport, it is only natural that Vancouver should have its own maritime museum. The key attraction is the ***Saint-Roch***, the first boat to circle North America by navigating the Panamá Canal and the Northwest Passage.

Get back on Chestnut Street and turn right on Cornwall Avenue, which becomes a scenic road named Point Grey Road.

You will now pass through **Kitsilano** *(between Arbutus and Alma Sts.)*, bordered to the north by a public beach. This area, whose wooden Queen Anne and Western Bungalow Style houses are typical of the West Coast, was a middle-class neighbourhood in the early 20th century. If you want to leave no stone unturned during your tour of Kitsilano, take a left on MacDonald Street. Around number 2100, a lovely row of gabled houses, each with a veranda in front, forms a cohesive whole (1912).

Turn right on 6th Avenue, then right again on Bayswater Street.

Tatlow Court (2) *(1820 Bayswater St.)*, a group of neo-Tudor row houses built around a central court, is worth a quick look.

Turn left on Point Grey Road, then right on Alma Street, which leads to **Pioneer Park (3)**, home of the **Hasting Mills Store** *(1575 Alma St.)*. Built in 1865, this former general store is the oldest building in Vancouver. Originally located east of Gastown, near the city's first sawmill, it was transported here by boat in 1930 and then restored by the Native Daughters of British Columbia, a charitable organization, which, in spite of its name, has nothing to do with indigenous peoples.

Head south on Alma Street, then turn right on 4th Avenue.

Fourth Avenue runs alongside lovely **Jericho Beach Park (4)**, a green space and beach rolled into one at the edge of English

Bay. Turn right on North West Marine Drive, then left on Belmont Avenue to see some of the loveliest houses on the peninsula. After, return to Northwest Marine Drive and head west to **Point Grey ★★★ (5)**, also known as Pacific Spirit Park, which stretches out into the salt water, offering a full panoramic view of the Strait of Georgia.

The tour continues onto the grounds of the **University of British Columbia ★ (6)**, or UBC. The university was created by the provincial government in 1908, but it was not until 1925 that the campus opened its doors on this lovely site on Point Grey. An architectural contest had been organized for the site layout, but the First World War halted construction work, and it took a student demonstration denouncing government inaction in this matter to get the buildings completed. Only the library and the science building were executed according to the original plans. **Set Foot for UBC** *(May to Aug, free tours organized by students, ☎ 822-TOUR)*.

To this day, the UBC campus is constantly expanding, so don't be surprised by its somewhat heterogeneous appearance. There are a few gems however, including the **Museum of Anthropology ★★★ (7)** *($6, free admission Tue 5pm to 9pm; in the summer, every day 10am to 5pm, in the winter closed Mon and on Dec 25 and 26; 6393 NW Marine Dr.; from downtown, take bus #4 UBC or bus #10 UBC; ☎ 822-3825)* which is not to be missed both for the quality of native artwork displayed here, including totem poles, and for the architecture of Arthur Erickson. Big concrete beams and columns imitate the shapes of traditional native houses, beneath which have been erected immense totem poles gathered from former native villages along the coast and on the islands. Wooden sculptures and various works of art form part of the permanent exhibition.

On the edge of the West Mall is the **Asian Centre (8)** *(1871 West Mall)*, capped with a big pyramid-shaped metal roof, beneath which are the department of Asian studies and an exhibition centre. Behind the building is the magnificent **Nitobe Memorial Garden ★★** *($2.50 summer, free winter; mid-Mar to mid-Oct, every day 10am to 6pm; winter, Mon to Fri 10am to 2:30pm; ☎ 822-9666)*, which symbolically faces Japan, on the other side of the Pacific. Farther along, **First Nations House of Learning ★ (9)** is a community centre for native students that was completed in 1993. It was designed to be a modern

EXPLORING

version of a Coast Salish Longhouse. The curved roof evokes the spirit of a bird (Larry Macfarland, architect). Totem poles surround the great hall, which can accommodate up to 400 people at a time.

The southwestern edge of the campus harbours a spot unlike any other, **Wreck Beach ★** *(NW Marine Dr. at University St.)*, where students come to enjoy some of life's pleasures. Nudists have made this their refuge, as have sculptors, who exhibit their talents on large pieces of driftwood. Vendors hawk all sorts of items next to improvised fast-food stands. A long stairway, that is quite steep in places, leads down to the beach.

EXCURSIONS OUTSIDE VANCOUVER

Among the many reasons to appreciate Vancouver, one in particular stands out. Unlike certain cities, where nearby suburbs are often the only place to get away for the weekend, Vancouver offers a wide choice of nearby destinations: **Whistler**, **Vancouver Island** and the **Gulf Islands** are the most famous.

Whistler (one day)

Whistler and **Blackcomb Mountains** *(hotel reservations: ☎ 932-4222, from Vancouver ☎ 685-3650, from the US ☎1-800-634-9622)* together make up the largest skiing area in Canada. As previously mentioned, these mountains have much to offer in the winter (see p 138 in "Outdoor Activities"). In the summer, a one day excursion to Whistler can also be very pleasant, with its countless boutiques and restaurants. Prices are sometimes high, however. A place for hat lovers: **The Hat Gallery** *(☎ 938-6695)* sells local creations and receives orders from as far away as Switzerland. Come nightfall, the town rocks to rhythms emanating from a dozen nightclubs. In the summer, the Vancouver Symphony Orchestra plays at the top of **Whistler Mountain** *(☎ 604-932-3434)* in the midst of unbelievable scenery.

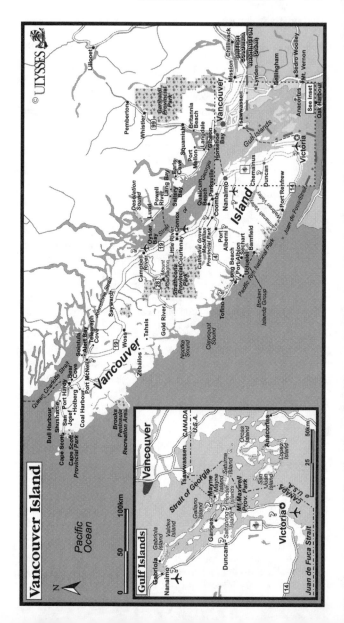

Getting To Whistler

By train: with **B.C. Rail** *(in Vancouver, ☎ 984-5246)* from North Vancouver.
By bus: **Maverick Coach Lines** *(in Vancouver, ☎ 662-8051)* offers several departures from Vancouver daily.
By car: via **Highway 99 North**. Vancouver: 120 kilometres, 2 hours 15 minutes; Kamloops: 400 kilometres, 5.5 hours; Seattle, WA: 338 kilometres, 5 hours.

Vancouver Island

Victoria (one or two days)

Victoria is a very British city. Many symbols from old England give it a particularly captivating charm. Anglophiles and the British will feel at home walking along **Government Street** and the **Port**. Buildings from the beginning of the century confer a particular style to this modern city. Among these are the **Parliament Buildings** and the shops, the most characteristic of which is the Morris Tobacconist Store, where you can still light up a cigar just like in the good old days. For the ultimate British experience, visitors can have tea in the majestic setting of the **Empress Hotel** *(☎ 250-384-8111)*. Reservations are recommended. Victoria's historic charm is further emphasized by its numerous buildings by the water, actually listed as historic monuments, such as the **Market Square**, which houses 40 original and colourful boutiques. Nearby, **Chinatown** has opted for this 19th-century district with winding alleys to set up its restaurants and shops. Victoria is not only nostalgic; besides the tattoo shops and health food stores, its development and "hippie-environmentalist" influence have spawned cybercafés like the **Mocambo Café** *(☎ 250-384-4468)*, where everyone surfs the Net at their leisure. A touch esoteric, local art is notably displayed at the **MacPherson Theatre** and the **Art Gallery of Greater Victoria**. Tarot-card fans can meet specialized readers at the **Avallon Metaphysical Centre** *(☎ 250-380-1721)*. Victoria is one of the loveliest seaside cities. A stroll along **Dallas Sunken Road** and **Beach Drive** is highly recommended. Here, opulent houses graced with gardens rival small rocky cliffs, and the view of the **Juan de Fuca Strait** is magnificent. To the north, the towns of **Oak Bay** and **Cadboro Bay** offer beautiful scenery along the

Canada Goose

beaches. Twenty minutes outside of Victoria is the enchanting countryside, where a series of flowerbeds dot the landscape. You can make the most of it by having a picnic in **John Dean Park**, but the best-known place in town remains world-famous **Butchart Gardens** *(☎ 250-652-5256)*.

South Coast (one day)

Vancouver Island's south coast is studded with local art boutiques. Nature's influence is notably apparent in all forms of art here, and sculptures and paintings by First Nations artists are numerous. By going through **Duncan**, you can visit the **Cowichan Native Centre** *(☎ 746-4636)*. The guided tour illustrates the way of life of native people: their customs and constructions. A very beautiful film is also presented; an art gallery and totems allow visitors to learn more about indigenous art.

In **Qualicum Beach**, the **Brant Festival** *(☎ 250-248-4117)* marks the return of thousands of geese in the spring, in April. Farther north, Campbell River lures steelhead and salmon fishing buffs.

EXPLORING

West Coast

On the island's west coast, the hundred-year old temperate rain forests and beaches skirting the cliffs are frequented by amateur and professional naturalists alike. Whale-watching excursions leave from Tofino. In Long Beach, waves crest as high as eight metres in the winter along the spectacular 15-kilometre-long beach. Dedicated hikers will enjoy the **West Coast Trail**, in the **Pacific Rim National Park**, which takes from five to seven days to cover *(reservations required, ☎ 663-6000 from Vancouver)*. Other hidden ecological treasures on this island include the **Carmanah Valley**, a forest of giant thousand-year old trees, the wild fjord of **Clayoquot Sound** and **Walbran Valley** *(B.C. Parks: ☎ 250-387-5002)*, a new provincial park where old Sitka spruce trees stand almost 100 metres tall. For further details, contact **Tourism Victoria** *(☎ 1-800-663-3883)* or the **Tourism Association of Vancouver Island** *(☎ 250-382-3551)*.

Getting Vancouver Island

B.C. Ferries *(☎ 1-888-223-3779)* offer several daily departures from Tsawwassen and Horseshoe Bay. By seaplane, **Air B.C.** *(Vancouver, ☎ 688-5515)* and **Harbour Air** *(☎ 1-800-663-4267)* fly from one downtown area to another. By helicopter, **Helijet** *(Vancouver, ☎ 273-1414)* also provides transportation to this area.

The Gulf Islands (two to four days)

These natural islands have retained their wild essence and charm by not being overly commercially developed: no concrete and few cars mar their beauty. These islands constitute havens of peace for stressed-out Vancouverites and hippies alike.

Salt Spring Island

Salt Spring is the most touristy of the Gulf Islands, with many art galleries, restaurants and boutiques. During the summer, artists and artisans flood the streets, exhibiting their work.

Throughout the island, "Studio" signs line the streets, indicating that is it possible to visit artists in their studios. Salt Spring Island boasts over 75 bed and breakfasts, hotels and log cabins by the water. For further details, contact the **Salt Spring Island Visitor Information Centre** *(☎ 250-537-5252)*.

Mayne Island

Unlike Salt Spring, Mayne does nothing to court tourists. Roadsigns are virtually non-existent. It is therefore recommended that you study the only public road map, set up near the harbour. Only a few remaining historic buildings testify to the island's past role as a prison; then it was nicknamed Little Hell. Relics confirm the island was once a colonial outpost with old trading posts and shops; the old **Mayne Inn Hotel** *(☎ 250-539-3122)*, with its period architecture, remains intact. For provisions and camping or hiking gear, **Miners Trading Post** *(☎ 250-539-2214)*, in the village of **Fernhill**, is a good bet. You can purchase good organic fruits and vegetables at the **Mayne Open Market** *(☎ 250-539-5024)*, locally known as MOM. The **Arbutus Deer Farm** *(☎ 250-539-2301)* sells venison and beef for barbecues. **Bennett Bay Beach** is a lovely place for a stroll. Both **Hanna Air** *(☎ 1-800-665-2359)* and **Harbour Air** *(☎ 1-800-665-0212)* offer direct flights between Vancouver and Mayne Island.

Pender Islands

Linked by a wooden bridge, the two Pender Islands, much like Mayne, are very quiet and their inhabitants do not like to be disturbed. Visitors come here especially to go bike riding and stroll along the long stretch of **beaches**. Mount Normand has a good reputation among hikers. The summit offers a unique view of the San Juan Islands. The "hippie-cool" ambiance of these islands is obvious; natural food stores and organic produce farms are prevale here. Try the **Southridge Farms Country Store** *(☎ 250-629-2051)* for organic fruits and vegetables. Sample excellent cuisine at the **Bedwell** restaurant *(☎ 250-629-3212)* or enjoy a beer at the **Port Browning Marina** pub *(☎ 250-629-3493)*, where local musicians often get together for jam nights. Bed and breakfasts ensure accommodation. For further information, write to the **South Pender Island B & B**

EXPLORING

(9956 Boundary Pass Dr., R.R. 1, Pender Island, VON 2M0), or call the **Canadian Gulf Islands B & B Association** *(☎ 250-539-5390)* for free accommodation and adventure-package bookings.

Galiano Island

The first thing you will notice upon arriving in Galiano is the scarcity of infrastructure and commercial development. The inhabitants' passionate protests to protect the ecological balance have attracted worldwide attention. Their efforts have enabled Galiano to preserve its vast stretches of great natural landscapes. The island also has many meditation centres and retreats for New Age enthusiasts, such as **Serenity By-the-Sea** *(☎ 1-800-944-2655)*.

The **Galiano Planet Revival Festival of Music** *(☎ 250-539-5778 for information)*, featuring indigenous dance performances and a varied repertoire of folk, jazz and funk offered by local artists, takes place in the summer. Not to be missed! Galiano also boasts many bed and breakfasts and rustic cabins for rent, as well as **campsites** in **Montague Harbour** *(☎ 250-539-2115)*. There is also a good selection of restaurants here, including **La Berengerie** *(☎ 250-539-5392)*, renowned for its Algerian food and lamb chops; it is also a bed and breakfast. Do not forget to bring bottled water as Galiano has no running water. Call **Galiano Getaways** *(☎ 250-539-5551 for B & B reservations)*. They also offer adventure packages; for more information, call the **Galiano Island Chamber of Commerce** *(☎ 250-539-2233)*.

Saturna Island

Saturna is perhaps the most isolated and least accessible of the Gulf Islands, and its inhabitants are determined to keep it that way. It has very limited facilities and only two restaurants. Nevertheless, there are many good reasons to visit the island. Nature lovers will be fascinated by its unusual fauna and flora, like the **giant mushrooms** at the base of **Mount Warburton**. On Canada Day (July 1st), a great annual lamb barbecue is organized. It is the largest local gathering of the year on the island. **Saturna Lodge** *(☎ 250-539-2254)* is one of the few inns here. Camping is forbidden on Saturna. For more information on accommodations, call ☎ 250-539-2930. To get to Saturna Island: **B.C. Ferries** *(☎ 1-888-223-3779)*. Reservations are essential during the summer.

OUTDOORS

Located where the mountains meet the sea, a short distance from the wilds of British Columbia, Vancouver offers an extremely wide range of outdoor activities. Downhill skiing, hiking in the woods, hang-gliding, salt-water swimming in the Strait of Georgia, sun-bathing on sandy beaches, sailboarding and surfing can all be enjoyed just a half-hour or less from downtown.

The ski resorts of the Coast Mountains, north of Vancouver, are easily accessible by car via the Lions Gate Bridge. They boast substantial vertical drops (over 1000 metres), and there is year-round cable car service to scenic lookouts on various mountaintops, from which visitors can take in outstanding views of the city. To the south, the beaches flanking the central neighbourhoods mean Vancouverites can go swimming in the ocean without leaving town — and the water isn't as polluted as you might think! Among the other popular activities, cycling and jogging in Stanley Park have become something of a ritual for many of the city's residents.

The local sports mania doesn't end there, however. Within the past few years, the city has built some impressive facilities for professional sports like football, hockey and most recently, basketball. This last sport, much more popular in the United

States than in Canada, is indicative of the growing influence of American culture here in Vancouver.

For general information on all outdoor activities in the Greater Vancouver area, contact **Sport B.C.** *(509-1367 Broadway, Vancouver, V6H 4A9, ☎ 737-3000)* or the **Outdoor Recreation Council of B.C.** *(334-1367 Broadway, Vancouver, V6H 4A9, ☎ 737-3058)*. Both organizations offer many suggestions and information.

Vancouver Parks & Recreation: *(☎ 257-8400)* provides all information on sports and recreation activities.

Altus Mountain Gear *(137 W. Broadway, ☎ 876-5255)*. Everything for the mountains: waterproof gear, clothing, tents, backpacks... Rental and some articles sold at cost.

Recreation Rentals *(2560 Arbutus St., Kitsilano, ☎ 733-7368)* offers everything for outdoor activities: camping equipment, tents, bicycles, skis, roller-blades, snowboards, canoes and kayaks.

 # BEACHES

The Vancouver shoreline is made up in large part of easily accessible sandy beaches. All these beaches lie along English Bay, where it is possible to walk, cycle, play volleyball and, of course, take a dip in the sea to fully enjoy the setting. Stanley Park is fringed by **Third Beach** and **Second Beach**, and then, farther east, along Beach Avenue, by **First Beach** where, on January 1, hundreds of bathers brave the icy water to celebrate the new year. A little farther east, **Sunset Beach** celebrates the day's end with gorgeous sunsets. At the southern edge of English Bay are **Kitsilano Beach**, **Jericho Beach**, **Locarno Beach**, **Spanish Banks Beach**, **Tower Beach** and, finally, **Wreck Beach** at the western edge of the University of British Columbia campus.

Kitsilano Beach is enlivened by beach volleyball tournaments and by an assortment of sports facilities, including a basketball court. Locarno, Jericho and Spanish Banks beaches are quieter spots for family relaxation where walking and reading are key activities.

OUTDOOR ACTIVITIES

 Hiking

Stanley Park is definitely the best place go hiking in Vancouver, with over 50 kilometres of trails through forest and greenery along the sea- and lakeshores, including the **Seawall**, an outstanding eight-kilometre trail flanked by giant trees.

If you like gardens and are heading through Chinatown, you won't need a pair of hiking boots to visit the **Dr. Sun Yat-Sen Classical Chinese Garden** (☎ 689-7133), whose little bridges and trails will guide you through a realm of peace and serenity (see "Exploring", p 72).

There are lots of places to go walking in the Point Grey area. Myriad trails crisscross the campus of the **University of British Columbia** (UBC). One of the best known runs across the famous **Endowment Lands**, **Pacific Spirit Park**, which cover an area twice as large as Stanley Park. Others lead to the **UBC Botanical Gardens** *(summer $4.50; winter free; mid-Mar to mid-Oct, every day 10am to 6pm; winter, everyday 10am to 2:30pm; 6804 SW Marine Dr., ☎ 822-9666)*: the **Botanical**, **Alpine**, **Native**, **Physic**, **Food**, **Contemporary** , **Asian** and **Winter** gardens, which are all linked by well-marked paths, and the **Nitobe Memorial Garden** (see "Exploring, p 109). There is also a whole network of trails through the forest, and since UBC is located on a peninsula, all trails ultimately lead to the beach.

On the other side of Lions Gate Bridge, in North Vancouver, Capilano Road leads to **Capilano Park** (☎ 432-6350), where you'll find a trail offering sweeping views of the Capilano River. During summer, you can see the salmon swimming upriver.

Mountain hiking can be done on one of the peaks near the city centre. **Cypress Provincial Park** (☎ 924-2200) north of the municipality of West Vancouver, has several hiking trails, among them the Howe Sound Crest Trail, which leads to different mountains including The Lions and Mount Brunswick. The views over the west shore of Howe Sound are really quite spectacular. You must wear good shoes and bring food for

OUTDOORS

these hikes. To get to Cypress Park by the Lion's Gate Bridge, follow the signs west along the TransCanada Highway and take the Cypress Bowl Road exit. Take the time to stop at the lookout to contemplate Vancouver, the Strait of Georgia and, on a clear day, Mount Baker in the United States.

The hike up **Grouse Mountain ★★★** *(☎ 984-0661)* is not particularly difficult, but the incline is as steep as 25° in places, so you have to be in good shape. It takes about two hours to cover the three-kilometre trail, which starts at the parking lot for the cable car. The view of the city from the top of the mountain is fantastic. If you are too tired to hike back down, take the cable car for the modest sum of five dollars.

Mount Seymour Provincial Park *(☎ 986-2261)* is another good hiking locale, offering two different views of the region. To the east is Indian Arm, a large arm of the sea extending into the valley.

A little farther east in this marvellous mountain range on the north shore, magnificent **Lynn Headwaters Park ★★★** is scored with forest trails. It is best known for its footbridge, which stretches across an 80-metre-deep gorge. Definitely not for the faint of heart! To get there, take Highway 1 from North Vancouver to the Lynn Valley Road exit and follow the signs, then turn right on Peters Road.

Lighthouse Park, in West Vancouver, is well suited to hiking on flatter terrain. From this site, you will be facing the University of British Columbia, the entrance to English Bay, and the Strait of Georgia. Take the Lion's Gate Bridge and follow Marine Drive West, crossing the city of West Vancouver and hugging the seashore until you reach the western edge of English Bay. Turn left at Beacon Lane toward Lighthouse Park.

If you get off the 99 just after the affluent suburb of West Vancouver and head west to Horseshoe Bay, you'll come to lovely little **Whytecliff Park**, located on the seashore. Most people come here to go picnicking or scuba diving. For an interesting little excursion, follow the rocky trail out to **Whyte Island** at low tide. Before heading out to this big rock, make sure to check what time the tides are due to come in, or you'll end up with wet feet.

Deer

A 15-minute **ferry** *(BC Ferry, ☎ 277-0277)* ride from Horseshoe Bay transports you to **Bowen Island ★★★** *(☎ 947-2216)*, where hiking trails lead through a lush forest. Although you'll feel as if you're at the other end of the world, downtown Vancouver is only 5 km away as the crow flies.

 Cycling

The region has a multitude of trails for mountain biking. Just head to one of the mountains north of the city. A pleasant eight-kilometre ride runs along the Seawall in Stanley Park. Bicycle rentals are available at **Stanley Park Rentals** *(1798 W. Georgia St., corner of Denman, ☎ 688-5141)*. Outside Vancouver, you can go cycling in the Fraser Valley, near farms or along secondary roads.

Heading away from Stanley Park on the **Seawall** from English Bay, you'll reach another seawall, which is less crowded and better for cycling. About 15 kilometres long, it skirts **False Creek**, passes in front of the recently built housing complex on the grounds of the 1986 World Fair, invites cyclists to stop in at Science World, leads to the markets on Granville Island, and finally ends up back at the starting point on English Bay via the Burrard Bridge. More courageous visitors can follow the **Spanish Banks** beach all the way to UBC. You have to ride along roads during certain parts of the trip. To avoid getting

OUTDOORS

lost, follow the green and white signs specifically posted for cyclists.

The 15-minute ferry ride from Horseshoe Bay out to little **Bowen Island** ★★★ *(☎ 947-2216)* is a worthwhile excursion. This perfectly lovely residential island has a network of quiet little country roads. You are likely to come across a deer or two, and make sure to keep an eye out for eagles soaring overhead. After a day of pedalling, you can enjoy a relaxing drink by the harbour at Snug Cove.

Bird-Watching

Birders should make a trip to the **George C. Reifel Bird Sanctuary** ★★ *(5191 Robertson Road, Delta, ☎ 946-6980)* on Westham and Reifel islands (see p 106). Dozens of species of migratory and non-migratory birds draw orinthology enthusiasts year-round to see aquatic birds, birds of prey, and many other varieties. Farther south, several species can also be observed at Boundary Bay and Mud Bay, as well as on Iona Island closer to Vancouver, next to the airport.

Bald Eagle

If you get off highway 99 just after the affluent suburb of West Vancouver and head west to Horseshoe Bay, you'll come to lovely little **Whytecliff Park**, located on the seashore. Keep your ears tuned and your eyes peeled and you will probably spot some bald eagles in the tops of the tallest trees.

The largest bald eagle population in the world is found just 60 kilometres from Vancouver, in **Brackendale**, which lies alongside the 99 on the way to Whistler. Winter is a particularly good time to visit. Eagle buffs mingle at the **Brackendale Art Gallery** *(P.O. Box 100, Brackendale, VON 1TO, ☎ 898-3333)*.

 Windsurfing

The pleasures afforded by the sea in Vancouver are definitely not to be taken lightly. **Howe Sound**, located alongside Highway 99 North on the way to Squamish, was slated to become a major harbour for giant freighters, but, to the great relief of local windsurfers, never did. The wind rushes into the hollow formed by the mountains on either side of the fjord, making this part of British Columbia a paradise for high-speed sailboarding. You can obtain all the necessary information about where to go at the **Squamish tourist office** *(37950 Cleveland Avenue, ☎ 892-9244)*. To find out about wind conditions, call the **Windtalker Windline** *(☎ 926-9463)*. A ten dollar fee covers insurance and potential rescue costs.

 Sea Kayaking

Like the mountains, the water is a key part of life in Vancouver, and there is an almost unlimited number of ways to get out and enjoy the sea. One option is to tour the city by sea kayak. **False Creek** stretches all the way to Main Street and Science World, and you'll pass Granville Island along the way; by paddling around **Stanley Park**, you can reach Canada Place and the skyscrapers downtown. More courageous visitors can set out along **Indian Arm ★★★** to Deep Cove, an expedition likely to include a few encounters with seals and eagles. Kayak rentals are available at **Ecomarine Ocean Kayak Centre**

OUTDOORS

(1668 Duranleau Street, Granville Island, ☎ 689-7575) on **Granville Island**.

 ## Canoeing and Kayaking

Those who prefer running white water on smaller crafts can contact one of the following agencies, which organize expeditions and will equip you from head to toe: **Whitewater Kayaking Association of B.C.** *(1367 Broadway, Vancouver, V6H 4A9, ☎ 222-1577)*, **Canoe Sport B.C.** *(3135 Richmond St., Richmond, V7E 2V4, ☎ 275-6651)* or **Canadian Adventure Tours** *(Box 929, Whistler, V0N 1B0, ☎ 938-0727)* (a good place if you're passing through Whistler).

Canadian River Expeditions *(301-3524 W. 16th Ave., Vancouver, V6R 3C1, ☎ 938-6651)* allows you to plan an expedition from Vancouver.

Sage Wilderness Experiences *(3-1370 Main St., North Vancouver, ☎ 938-3103)* is yet another place, located near Vancouver's North Shore.

Sea To Sky Trails *(105C-11831 80th Ave., Delta, V4C 7X6, ☎ 594-7701)* is a small adventure travel agency located in a suburb south of Vancouver .

The Great B.C. Adventure Company *(Box 39116, Vancouver, V6R 1G0, ☎ 730-0323)* is another such outfit, allowing you to further compare rates.

 ## Rafting

Thrill-seekers will certainly appreciate the waterways around Vancouver. A white-water rafting paradise awaits visitors in the heart of Cascade Mountains, a semi-arid region less than two hours away from the city by car, on **Fraser River**, the greatest waterway in British Columbia in terms of flow. Certain parts of the river are sure to make your hair stand on end.

Thompson River (a tributary of Fraser River) is the best-known for white-river rafting. This beautiful emerald green river runs through a magnificent rocky, arid landscape. Experts will tell you the Thompson River descent is a real roller-coaster ride. Good luck!

Coquihalla River is another interesting and worthwhile destination. This powerful little river runs at the bottom of a deep canyon offering spectacular scenery. Another tumultuous little river, the **Nahatlatch**, is less frequented than its renowned counterparts, but worth considering nonetheless. The river closest to Vancouver on which to go rafting is the **Chilliwack**. Despite its proximity to large urban centres, this river runs through a wild landscape. Over the course of the years, it has acquired a solid reputation among kayakers and canoeists.

Fraser River Raft Expeditions *(Box 10, Yale, V0K 2S0, ☎ 863-2336)* is located in the heart of the Fraser River canyon and specializes in expeditions on the Fraser, Thompson, Coquihalla and Nahatlatch Rivers.

Hyak Wilderness Adventures *(204B-1975 Maple St., Vancouver, V6J 3S9, ☎ 734-8622)* is a major rafting enterprise with an excellent reputation. It has the practical advantage of having its offices in Vancouver and offers expeditions on the Chilliwack, Fraser and Thompson Rivers.

REO Rafting Adventures *(☎ 684-4438)* is a big agency that organizes white-water rafting on the Chilliwack, Nahatlatch and Thompson Rivers. Group rates.

Ryan's Rapid Rafting *(Box 129, Spence's Bridge, V0K 2L0, ☎ 250-458-2479)*, a small, reliable outfit, located on the banks of Thompson River, offers expeditions on the Thompson and Chilliwack Rivers.

 ## Sailing

Going for a sail is the best way to visit some of the lovely spots in **Vancouver Harbour**. Jericho Beach, in the Kitsilano area, is an excellent starting point. You can rent your own sailing dinghy or Hobie Cat at the **Jericho Sailing Centre Association** *(1300 Discovery Street, ☎ 731-5415)*, or climb aboard a larger sailboat for a cruise of several hours or several days. The

OUTDOORS

Cooper Boating Centre *(1620 Duranleau Street, Granville Island,* ☎ *687-4110)* is a good place to keep in mind.

Pleasure Boating

Renting an outboard **motor boat** is as easy as renting a car. No special permit is required for you to putter around at your leisure or speed across the water, as long as you stay near the shore. You'll find everything you need at **Granville Island Boat Rentals** *(16296 Duranleau Street, Granville Island,* ☎ *682-6287)*.

Fishing

Salt-Water Fishing

Vancouver is the starting point for unforgettable fishing. When it comes to sea fishing, **salmon** reigns supreme. Before casting your line, you must obtain a permit from a specialized outfitter, from whom you can also rent out the necessary equipment: they have boats, know the best locations, supply equipment and often meals, too. Make sure you are dressed appropriately, though. Even when the sun is out, it can get very cold on the open sea. It is also essential that you not forget your fishing permit. You will find a mine of information in *BC Sportsfishing* magazine *(contact Rick Taylor, 909 Jackson Crescent, New Westminster, V3L 4S1,* ☎ *683-4871,* ≈ *683-4318)*.

A-Wild West Salmon Charters *(34B W. 19th Ave., Vancouver, V5Y 2B2,* ☎ *443-7802)*. Salmon fishing in Vancouver, near the Capilano estuary, from June to October.

Coho Sports *(4152 Penticton St.,* ☎ *435-7333,* ≈ *435-7333)* offers salmon fishing in such regions as the Sunshine Coast. Trips depart from Vancouver, last half a day to four days, and include meals. Coho Sports also provides apartments for those who opt for longer stays. All fishing gear is supplied.

Black Gold Lodge *(3826 Azalea Pl., Port Coquitlam,* ☎ *941-3228)* offers not only accommodation but boat rentals and sea-fishing gear as well.

West Coast Fishing Resorts *(4680 Crowley Crescent, Richmond, V7B 1C1, ☎ 278-3130 or ☎ 1-800-810-8933, ≈ 278-3120,)* is a large salmon fishing centre with three sea fishing camps at which you can stay: Whale Channel, Milbanke and Sound River Inlet. Open from May to September.

Westing Bayshore Yacht Charters *(1601 W. Georgia St, ☎ 691-6936)* has an impressive fleet of fishing yachts.

Fresh-Water Fishing

With an infinite number of lakes and rivers, trout fishing in British Columbia is always excellent. Permits are sold in all camping equipment stores as well as at **Ruddik's Fly Fishing** *(1654 Duranleau St., Granville Island, ☎ 681-3747)*, a good shop for this sport. Thousands of flies for catching every kind of fish in the area can be purchased here. The owner will gladly offer advice. Vancouver is the starting point to equip yourself and make inquiries, though you will have to leave the city to fish on a river or lake. The interior region and Cariboo Country are prime destinations for anglers in Vancouver. You can also purchase an issue of *BC Sportsfishing* at almost any newsagent's or call on fishing clubs or outfitters. A few good outfitters are listed below. Many of these are located outside Vancouver, though they do have booking offices in the city so as to be accessible to their clientele.

N.B.   Salt-water and fresh-water fishing licenses are not interchangeable.

Pinantan Lake Family Resort *(3838 W. 22nd Ave., Vancouver, V6S 1J7, ☎ 222-2698, ≈ 222-2698)* is situated in Cariboo Country, four hours from Vancouver. As its name suggests, this establishment caters to families. Guests can spend the night in one of the charming little houses by the lake.

Located in Cariboo Country, the **Sheridan Lake Ranch** *(540-220 Cambie St., Vancouver, V6B 2M9, ☎ 250-593-4510)* offers fishing in the heart of nature. Boats, permits and equipment are supplied, and mountain bikes are for rent to explore the surrounding area. Visitors can also practise cross-country skiing here, as the ranch is open all year round.

OUTDOORS

The **Crazy Bear Lake Lodge** *(Box 34312, Vancouver, V6J 4P3,
☎ 739-0789, ⇔ 739-0789)* is open from June to September.
The owner speaks German, Spanish and English, of course.
Pets are welcome, and the fishing is excellent.

Open all year round, **Taseko Lake Lodge** *(204-814 W. 15th St.,
North Vancouver, V7P 1M6, ☎ 988-7143, ⇔ 988-7092)* offers
equipped log cabins that each can accommodate up to 12
people; meals are included. Canoes are available, and a guide
will take you to prime locations. Guests can also go horseback
riding here.

Situated in Cariboo Country, **Elkin Creek Guest Ranch** *(4462
Marion Rd., North Vancouver, V7K 2V2, ☎ 984-4666,
⇔ 984-4686)* offers 23 rooms and lodgings, nine of which have
running water, from April to October. The ranch can
accommodate up to 40 guests. Boats, permits and equipment
are provided. Since Elkin Creek is a ranch, guests can also
enjoy horseback riding here.

For more information on fresh water fishing, you can visit the
Granville Island Sport Fishing Museum (see p 100 in
"Exploring").

 ## Whale Watching

Visitors can admire great marine mammals on the outskirts of
Vancouver; including **grey whales**, **killer whales** and other
finbacks. There are observation boats on Vancouver Island.
Here are a few places that can help you plan your outing:

Bluewater Adventures: ☎ 980-3800

Seaker Adventure Tours: ☎ 1-800-728-0244

Stubbs Island Whale Watching *(Box 7, Dept. BCOA, Telegraph
Cove, V0N 3J0, ☎ 250-928-3185)* specializes in the
observation of killer whales. A hydrophone records the singing
of whales, and you can even keep the cassette.

Killer Whale

 Mountaineering

A trip to Vancouver without tackling the snow-covered peaks that surround the city would be a real shame. The **Federation of Mountain Clubs of B.C.** *(336-1367 Broadway, Vancouver, V6H 4A9, ☎ 737-3053)* is a very reliable club, with experienced instructors. Excursions are organized on a regular basis.

 Rock-Climbing

As you are aware, Vancouver is surrounded by mountains. On that account, rock-climbing sites are hardly lacking. One of the best known in western North America, **Squamish Chief**, lies 60 kilometres from Vancouver. This rock, at an altitude of 780 metres, is considered the second largest monolith in the world, after El Capitan in California. Squamish Chief boasts rock climbing routes: you have only to hook your karabiners.

Squamish Rock Guides *(Box 871, Squamish, ☎ 892-2086)*. This agency's guides will take you exploring Squamish Chief. Those who like granite will be well served.

OUTDOORS

Mescalito Adventure Company *(50639 O'Byrne, Chilliwack,* ☎ *858-2300)* will assist you in climbing the cliffs and mountains overlooking the Fraser Valley.

Helicopter Sightseeing

If Vancouver's scenery has already won you over, here is something that will truly take your breath away! A glacier-skimming helicopter ride over snow-covered peaks and turquoise lakes is a must. Some agencies even offer landings on the glaciers. Though somewhat pricey, you will have unforgettable memories and extraordinary photographs too.

Mountain Heli Sports *(4340 Sundial Crescent, Whistler,* ☎ *932-2070)* is a very versatile agency, offering not only flights over mountains and Vancouver, but heli-skiing as well.

Southern Mountain Helicopters *(104-5225 216th St., Langley, B.C., V3A 4R1,* ☎ *534-7918)* is located in the Vancouver suburbs, at the gateway to the Fraser Valley.

Tyax Heli-Skiing *(Box 849, Whistler, VON 1BO,* ☎ *932-7007)* is a very well-known agency in Whistler for heli-skiing.

Valley Helicopters *(63235 Flood-Hope Rd., R.R. 2, Hope, VOX 1LO,* ☎ *869-2131)*, at the gateway to the city of Hope, a stone's throw from TransCanada Highway 1, will take you flying over Mount Baker and Manning Provincial Park.

Vancouver Helicopters *(5455D Airport Rd. S., Richmond,* ☎ *270-1484)* is located right near Vancouver International Airport. This enterprise has a fine reputation and will take you anywhere you want.

Kite Flying

With its 26 kilometres of beaches, Vancouver is the perfect place to go fly a kite. The most renowned spot for this activity is **Vanier Park**, which borders the beaches on English Bay, behind the Vancouver Museum. To get there, take the Burrard Bridge out of the downtown area and follow Chestnut Street through the pretty neighbourhood of Kitsilano. If you need equipment, **Kite Horizon Aerosports** *(1807 Burrard Street,* ☎ *738-5867)* has an infinite array of kites, including some high-performance models.

 ## Horseback Riding

Horseback riding opportunities are virtually limitless around Vancouver, with many bridle paths along forest roads. Contact **Back Country Horsemen of B.C.** *(Fraser Valley,* ☎ *856-8276; Mission* ☎ *462-0464)*, which has representatives throughout British Columbia, or write to the provincial head office *(SS1, Site 5, Box 70, Cranbrook, V1C 6H3)*.

 ## In-Line Skating

In-line skating, more commonly known as rollerblading, is a standard summer activity in Vancouver. Although you'll see skaters all over, the most popular place to go is around Stanley Park, on the **Seawall**, a fantastic eight-kilometre trail flanked by a century-old forest. Skate rentals are available at many places along the beach, including and **Outa-Lines Inlines** *(1231 Pacific Boulevard,* ☎ *899-2257)*.

 ## Golf

Vancouver is unquestionably the golf capital of Western Canada, with golf for all tastes and budgets. Golf courses in Vancouver and its surrounding areas are virtually all hilly and offer spectacular views of the ocean and especially the mountains, which loom over all parts of the region. It should be noted that all golf clubs require appropriate attire. For lack of space, there are very few courses in Vancouver itself, but the suburbs boast one at practically every turn.

The **University Golf Club** *(5185 University Blvd.,* ☎ *224-1818)* is one of the best-known in town and among the priciest. It is situated a stone's throw from the University of British Columbia (UBC). Sean Connery has played here.

OUTDOORS

The oldest public golf course, the **Peace Portal Golf Course** *(16900 4th Avenue, Surrey, ☎ 538-4818)* was founded in 1928 and is open year-round. It lies along Highway 99, near the U.S. border, in the suburb of Surrey.

In Richmond, another of the city's southern suburbs, the **Mayfair Lakes Golf and Country Club** *(5460 No. 7 Road, Richmond)* has a top-notch green surrounded by water.

No golf course boasts a more spectacular setting than **Furry Creek** *(P.O. Box 1000, Lions Bay, ☎ 922-9576 or 922-9461)*, located just past the village of Lions Bay, on **Howe Sound**, which Highway 99 North runs alongside on its way to Squamish. Nestled away in a splendid landscape, this course is more than just pleasant; imagine the sea stretched out beside towering, snow-capped peaks. Amazing.

The **Fraserview Golf Course** *(7800 Vivian Dr., ☎ 327-5616)* is an affordable golf course, managed by the city (Vancouver Board of Parks and Recreation Public Course) and located at the southern tip of Vancouver.

The **Langara Golf Course** *(6706 Alberta St., ☎ 257-8355)* is also a municipal golf course (Vancouver Board of Parks and Recreation Public Course), situated southeast of town.

Gleneagles *(6190 Marine Dr., West Vancouver, ☎ 921-7353)*, right near the lovely village of Horseshoe Bay and 15 minutes from Vancouver, is a very inexpensive golf course that is sometimes jam-packed on weekends, but the scenery makes playing here worth the wait.

In North Vancouver, in a very mountainous region, is the **Seymour Golf and Country Club** *(3723 Mt. Seymour Pkwy, North Vancouver, ☎ 929-2611)*. Oddly enough, this club is only open to the public Mondays through Fridays.

The **Burnaby Mountain Golf Club** *(7600 Halifax, Burnaby, ☎ 280-7355)* is located in a lovely setting, close to Simon Fraser University (SFU), 15 minutes east of Vancouver.

The **Riverway Golf Course** *(9001 Riverway Pl., Burnaby, ☎ 280-4653)* is another beautiful golf course in Burnaby, though it's a little remote.

In Coquitlam, a suburb northeast of Vancouver, is the **Westwood Plateau Golf & Country Club** *(3251 Plateau Blvd., Coquitlam, ☎ 552-0777)*, a brand new golf course with spectacular scenery and grounds. Be advised, however, that the golf marshal is not overly fond of slow players and, considering the $95 admission fee, you had best be a fine player!

Whistler Golf Clubs

Whistler golf courses have an excellent reputation, but playing here is hardly a bargain. These courses, of course, are closed throughout the winter because of snow. This is not the case for those in Vancouver and its suburbs, which are accessible all year long. Those keen enough to drive two hours out of Vancouver can check out the following places.

The course at the **Nicklaus North Golf Club** *(Whistler, ☎ 938-9898)* course was designed by none other than the famous golf champion, Jack Nicklaus.

The **Chateau Whistler Golf Club** *(4612 Blackcomb Way, Whistler, ☎ 938-2090)* is part of the Canadian Pacific holiday resort complex. The ultimate in luxury!

The **Whistler Golf Club** *(4010 Whistler Way, ☎ 932-5538)* is a little less expensive than the Chateau club.

Driving Ranges in Vancouver and Surrounding Areas

University Golf Club: 5185 University Boulevard, ☎ 224-1818

Musqueam Golf Club: 3904 West 51st Avenue, ☎ 266-2334

Seymour Golf and Country Club: 3723 Mt. Seymour Parkway, North Vancouver, ☎ 929-2611

Riverway Golf Course: 9001 Riverway Place, Burnaby, ☎ 280-4653

Westwood Plateau Golf & Country Club: 3251 Plateau Boulevard, Coquitlam, ☎ 552-0777

OUTDOORS

Mayfair Lakes Golf Course: 5460 No. 7 Road, Richmond, ☎ 276-0505

Pitch & Putt

Pitch & Putt is a simplified version of golf. Although the rules are quite similar, you don't necessarily have to be a practiced golfer to play. For about twelve dollars per person (equipment included), you can spend a pleasant day with your friends or family outside amidst flowers and impeccable greenery. Vancouver has three Pitch & Putt courses, the best known being the one in **Stanley Park** *(c/o Parks Office, 2099 Beach Avenue, ☎ 681-8847)*. The other two are in **Queen Elizabeth Park** *(☎ 874-8336)*, which stretches south of town, and **Rupert Park** *(3402 Charles St., ☎ 257-8364)*, to the east.

Health Clubs

If you are a member of a gym in your own country or home town, **your card could be accepted in Vancouver**. Many clubs, in fact, are part of international organizations. Check whether your card is valid by contacting your club or those in Vancouver. Those listed below are all located in the Vancouver area.

The **Bentall Centre Athletic Club** *(Bentall 4, 1055 Dunsmuir St., ☎ 689-4424)* is a typical business club, located in the business district.

Denman Fitness Company *(1731 Comox St., ☎ 688-2484)* is a small and very pleasant neighbourhood sports club with many gay members.

The **Fitness Quest Gym** *(444 W. 6th Ave., ☎ 879-7855)* is a well-equipped independent club.

Fitness World *(1214 Howe St., ☎ 681-3232)* is part of the biggest chain of health clubs in Vancouver.

Fitness World *(1989 Marine Dr., North Vancouver, ☎ 986-3487)* is the largest and poshest link in the Fitness World chain. An absolute must. Easy parking.

Fitness World *(555 W. 12th Ave., ☎ 876-1009)*. Here is another Fitness World. This one is ultra-high-tech and sometimes jam-packed at the end of the day.

Olympic Athletic Club *(2627 Arbutus St., ☎ 736-2308)*. Far to the west of the city, this club has an excellent reputation.

As its name suggests, **RZ Lady Sport** *(1681 Chestnut, ☎ 737-4355)* caters only to women.

RZ Sports Club *(200-1807 W. 1st Ave., ☎ 737-4355)*. Situated a stone's throw from RZ Lady Sport, this gym is mixed.

Cross-Country Skiing

Less than a half-hour from Vancouver, three ski resorts welcome snow-lovers from morning to evening. In **Cypress Provincial Park**, on **Hollyburn Ridge ★**, Cypress Bowl Ski Areas *(☎ 926-5612)* offers 25 kilometres of mechanically maintained trails suitable for all categories of skiers. These trails are frequented day and evening by cross-country skiers. There are also trails at **Grouse Mountain** *(☎ 984-0661)* and **Mount Seymour Provincial Park** *(☎ 986-2261)*.

Downhill Skiing

What makes Vancouver a truly magical place is the combination of sea and mountains. The cold season is no exception, as residents desert the beaches and seaside paths to crowd the ski hills, which are literally suspended over the city. There are four ski resorts close to the city: **Mount Seymour** *(adults $26; 1700 Mount Seymour Rd., North Vancouver, B.C., V7G 1L3; Upper Level Hwy. heading east, Deep Cove Exit, information ☎ 986-2261, ski conditions ☎ 879-3999, ☎ and ≈ 986-2267)*, a family resort with beginner trails, situated east of North Vancouver, above Deep Cove; **Grouse Mountain** *(adults $28; night skiing $20; 6400 Nancy*

OUTDOORS

Greene Way, North Vancouver, information ☎ 984-0661, ski conditions ☎ 986-6262, ski school ☎ 980-9311), a small resort accessible by cable car, which offers an unobstructed view of Vancouver that is as magnificent by day as it is by night; **Cypress Bowl** *(adults $33, night skiing $23; from North Vancouver, take TransCanada Highway 1, heading west for 16 km, then follow road signs. Information and ski conditions ☎ 926-5612)*, a resort for the most avid skiers, also offers magnificent views of Howe Sound and of the city. For more affordable skiing, try the village-style **Hemlock Valley Resort** *(adults $30, night skiing $11; Hwy. 1 heading east, Agassizou Harrisson Hot Springs Exit; information ☎ 797-4411, ski conditions ☎ 520-6222, ☎ 797-4440, accommodation reservations ☎ 797-4444)*. Situated at the eastern tip of Vancouver's urban area, in the heart of the Cascade Mountains, this resort boasts an abundance of snow and a spectacular view of Mount Baker in the United States. As soon as enough snow blankets the slopes, in late November or early December, these four ski resorts are open every day until late at night thanks to powerful neon lighting. It should be noted, however, that the first three resorts do not provide accommodation (consult Tour F: Burrard Inlet in the "Accommodations" chapter, p 146 for the nearest hotels).

Those who prefer skiing outside the metropolitan area can head to **Whistler**. This ski resort is considered the best in North America, with an annual snowfall of nine metres and a 1,600-metre vertical drop. There are two mountains to choose from: **Whistler Mountain** and **Blackcomb Mountain** *(hotel reservations, ☎ 1-604-932-4222; from Vancouver, ☎ 685-3650; from the US, ☎ 1-800-634-9622)*. The skiing here is extraordinary, and the facilities ultramodern — but mind your budget! You will understand why prices are so high upon seeing hordes of Japanese and American tourists monopolize the hotels and intermediate ski runs. Whistler and Blackcomb Mountains together make up the largest skiing area in Canada. These world-class, twin ski playgrounds are blessed with heavy snowfalls and boast enough hotels to house a city's entire population. This top-of-the-range ski metropolis also offers the possibility of gliding through pristine powder and, weather permitting, you will find yourself swooshing through an incredibly beautiful alpine landscape. **Whistler Mountain** *(adults $42; from Vancouver, Hwy. 99 heading north for 130 km, information ☎ 932-3434, ski conditions ☎ 932-4191)* is the elder of the two resorts. Experts, powderhounds and skijumpers will all flock to Peak Chair, the chair lift that leads to the top of Whistler Mountain. From its summit, diehard skiers and snowboarders have access to a ski area composed of blue (intermediate) and expert (black-diamond and double-diamond) trails, covered in deep fleecy snow. **Blackcomb Mountain** *(adults $44; in Whistler; from Vancouver, Hwy. 99 heading north for 130 km; 4545 Blackcomb Way, Whistler, B.C., VON 1B4; information ☎ 932-3141, ski conditions ☎ 932-4211)* is the "stalwart" skiing Mecca of ski buffs in North America. For years now, a fierce debate has been waged by skiers over which of the two mountains (Whistler or Blackcomb) is the best. One thing is certain, Blackcomb wins first place for its vertical drop of 1,609 metres. Check out the glacier at Blackcomb – it is truly magnificent!

N.B.: Snowboarding is permitted at all of these resorts.

ACCOMMODATIONS

Vancouver is a big city with lodgings for all tastes and budgets. All accommodations shown here are well located, within walking distance of bus stops and, in most cases, in or near the downtown area. **Super, Natural British Columbia** (☎ 1-800-663-6000) can make reservations for you.

Ulysses' Favourites

For romantic atmosphere: Hotel Vancouver (see p 146), Wedgewood Hotel (see p 142).

For its swimming pool: Westin Bayshore (see p 146).

For its lobby: Pan Pacific Hotel (see p 143).

For the view: Landmark Hotel (see p 145), Sylvia Hotel (see p 143).

CHINATOWN AND EAST VANCOUVER

Simon Fraser University *($48; sb, K, ℝ, ℙ; Room 212, McTaggart-Cowan Hall, Burnaby, ☎ 291-4503, ⇄ 291-5598).* This student residence is available from May to August and is located atop a mountain. If you bring a sleeping bag, a room for two costs about $40, saving you about $10. SFU is 20 kilometres east of downtown Vancouver.

 DOWNTOWN

YMCA *($39; sb, tv, K, ≈; 955 Burrard Street, ☎ 681-0221, ⇄ 681-1630).* This establishment on the corner of Nelson Street is not actually restricted to men, and families are welcome. The building is brand-new and offers rooms accommodating one to five persons.

Bosman's Motor Hotel *($139; ≡, pb, ≈, ℙ; 1060 Howe St., ☎ 682-3171).* In the heart of the city, close to the National Museum, theatres and beaches. The rooms are spacious and modern.

The **Wedgewood Hotel** *($240; pb, ⊘, △, ≡, ℜ; 845 Hornby St., V6Z 1V2, ☎ 689-7777, 1-800-663-0666, ⇄ 608-5348)* is small enough to have retained some character and style, in particular the lovely lobby complete with shiny brass accents, cosy fireplace and distinguished art, and large enough to offer a certain measure of privacy and professionalism. This is a popular option for business trips and romantic weekend getaways.

Canadian Pacific Waterfront Centre Hotel *($220-$350; tv, ≈, ⊘, ✗, ≡, △, ⊛, ℙ, ℜ, ♿; 900 Canada Place Way, ☎ 691-1991, ⇄ 691-1999)* is a Canadian Pacific luxury hotel located just a few steps from Gastown. It has 489 rooms.

Once a Delta hotel, the **Metropolitan Hotel** *($365; ⊘, ⊛, ≡, ✗, ♿, tv, ℜ, △, ≈, ℙ; 645 Howe St., ☎ 687-1122 or 1-800-667-2300, ⇄ 643-7267)* is located right downtown, just steps from the business district. These luxury accommodations

ACCOMMODATIONS

also have a luxurious price tag. The hotel's restaurant, Diva, with its pleasant staff and a cosy ambience, is worth trying.

 Pan Pacific Hotel Vancouver *($410; ≡, ◉, ☉, tv, ≈, △, ℙ, ℜ; 300-999 Canada Place, ☎ 662-8111, in Canada 1-800-663-1515 or in US 1-800-937-1515, ≈ 685-8690)* is a very luxurious hotel located in Canada Place, on the shore of Burrard Inlet facing North Vancouver, with a good view of port activities. During their visit to Vancouver in 1993, Russian President Boris Yeltsin and his entire entourage stayed at this hotel. It has 506 rooms. Its lobby, with its marble decor, 20-metre-high ceilings and panoramic view of the ocean, is magnificent.

THE WEST END

The **Barclay Hotel** *($75 bkfst incl.; tv, ℜ; 1348 Robson St., ☎ 688-8850, ≈ 688-2534)* is an older though spotless establishment with direct access to a pricey restaurant.

Buchan Hotel *($75 sb, $100 pb, children under 12 free; bicycle and ski racks, tv; 1906 Haro Street, ☎ 685-5354 or 1-800-668-6654, ≈ 685-5367)* is located in the West End residential area near Stanley Park beneath the trees. At the end of Haro Street, on Lagoon Drive, three municipal tennis courts are accessible to guests. Other tennis courts, a golf course and hiking trails can be found near this 61-room, three-story hotel. Smoking on the premises is prohibited.

Sylvia Hotel *($100; pb, tv, ℂ, ℜ, ✗, ℙ; 1154 Gilford Street, ☎ 681-9321)*. Located just a few steps from English Bay, this charming old hotel, built in the early 1900s, offers unspoiled views and has 118 simple rooms. People come for the atmosphere, but also for food and drink at the end of the day. For those on lower budgets, rooms without views are offered at lower rates. The manager of this ivy-covered hotel is a Frenchman who is fully and justifiably dedicated to his establishment. Request a southwest-facing room (one facing English Bay) in order to benefit from magical sunsets over the bay.

Oceanside *($700 per week, $1,500 per month; pb, tv, ; 1847 Pendrell St., ☎ 682-5641)*. Complete apartments, with separate bedrooms; right downtown, a walk away from the major attractions.

The affordable **Tropicana Motor Inn** *($129; tv, ℂ, ℜ, △, ≈; 1361 Robson St., ☎ 687-6631, ⇌ 687-5724)* rarely has the "no vacancy" sign up. A great location right in the action on the busy part of Robson probably has something to do with it. It is not a palace, but is perfect for younger travellers and people on a tighter budget.

The comfortable and simple luxuriousness of the **Riviera Motor Inn** *($148; tv, ℂ; 1431 Robson St., ☎ 685-1301, ⇌ 685-1335)* is nevertheless a bit expensive.

🏠 **West End Guest House Bed & Breakfast** *($150 bkfst incl.; pb, ℙ, ⊛, no children under 12; 1362 Haro Street, ☎ 681-2889, ⇌ 688-8812)*. This magnificent inn set in a turn-of-the-century Victorian house is well situated near a park and near Robson Street. Evan Penner is your host. A minimum two-day stay may apply, but not hesitate: the West End Guest House has an excellent reputation. (Nearby, at 1415 Barclay Street, is Roedde House, built in Victorian-Edwardian style in 1893 and designed by none other than the architect Francis Rattenbury, who also created the Vancouver Art Gallery, the legislature building in Victoria, and the Empress Hotel.)

The **Greenbrier Apartment Motor Hotel** *($159; tv, ℂ, ℜ; 1393 Robson St., ☎ 683-4558, ⇌ 669-3109)* is particularly popular with globetrotters. You'll meet world travellers who have decided to take a break in Vancouver. Ask about weekly and monthly rates.

The **Parkhill Hotel** *($160; tv, ◔, ℜ, △, ≈; 1160 Davie St., ☎ 685-1311 or 1-800-663-1525, ⇌ 681-0208)* is right in the middle of Vancouver's gay village. The rooms are perfectly comfortable and the restaurant serves fine Japanese cuisine. Just steps from English Bay and Stanley Park.

The **Blue Horizon Hotel** *($170; tv, ℜ, △, ≈, ≡, ⊛, ◔, ⚓; 1225 Robson St., ☎ 688-1411 or 1-800-663-1333, ⇌ 688-4461)* recently re-opened after extensive renovations. Each of the 214 rooms affords an exceptional view of the city.

Reasonably priced meals are served in the interior "granite" decor or out on the terrace facing Robson Street.

The **Robsonstrasse City Motor Inn** *($170; tv, C; 1394 Robson St.,* ☎ *687-1674 or 1-888-667-8877,* ≠ *685-7808)* is another affordable Robson Street option. The clientele is similar to that of the Tropicana (see above).

🏨 The **Landmark Hotel** *($200; tv, ⊛, ⊙, ℜ, △, ≈, ბ; 1400 Robson St.,* ☎ *687-0511 or 1-800-830-6144,* ≠ *687-2801)* truly is a landmark with it 40 floors and its revolving resto-bar at the top. The view is fascinating and quite an experience! The whole city unfolds before you in 90 minutes as the restaurant revolves 360°. The best time is at sunset when the sky darkens and the city seems to glow.

🏨 **Listel O'Doul's Hotel** *($200; tv, ℜ, △, ⊛, ბ; 1300 Robson St.,* ☎ *684-8461 or 1-800-663-5491,* ≠ *684-8326)* on Robson also houses a friendly, though slightly noisy, pub and a good restaurant. The service and comfort are indisputable.

Pacific Palisades Hotel *($225-$290; tv, ≈, P, ℜ, ℝ, C, ბ, ⊙; 1277 Robson Street,* ☎ *688-0461 or 1-800-663-1815,* ≠ *688-4374)* is part of the Shangri-La hotel chain. Its two towers, totalling 233 rooms, offer superb views of the sea and the mountains. Rooms facing north on the upper floors provide especially fine mountain views. A big pool and a well-equipped gymnasium are available to guests. All services for tourists or business travellers are looked after with professionalism. The staff are friendly and efficient.

🏨 **Sutton Place Hotel** *($265-$415; ⊛, ⊙, ≈, △, ℝ, ℜ, ბ; 845 Burrard Street,* ☎ *682-5511 or 1-800-961-7555,* ≠ *682-5513)*, formerly the Meridien, offers 397 rooms and the full range of five-star services normally provided by the top hotel chains. The European decor has been maintained. If you are a chocolate lover, don't miss the chocolate buffet served on Friday.

🏨 **Coast Plaza at Stanley Park** *($330; ≈, △, tv, ⊙, ℜ, C, ℝ, ✗, ბ, P; 1733 Comox Street,* ☎ *688-7711 or 1-800-663-1144,* ≠ *688-5934)*. If you are looking for a big, modern, American-style hotel close to the beach, this 267-room establishment is a good choice. The restaurant serves everything, and the food is decent.

 Hotel Vancouver *($330; tv, ≈, ®, ☉, △, ℜ, ℝ, ✕, ঌ, :P; 900 West Georgia Street, ☎ 684-3131 or 1-800-441-1414, ≈ 662-1929)* belongs to the Canadian Pacific Hotel chain and was built in the 1930s in the château style characteristic of Canadian railway hotels, of which the Château Frontenac in Québec City was a precursor. In 1939 it hosted George VI, the first British monarch to visit Canada. You will find tranquillity and luxury in the heart of downtown near Robson Street and Burrard Street. The hotel has 508 rooms.

STANLEY PARK

 The **Apricot Cat Guest House** *($95-$115 bkfst incl.; pb, tv; 628 Union St., ☎ 215-9898, ≈ 255-9271)* is a beautiful, old restored house that is just at the outer edge of downtown, not far from Stanley Park, the conference centre, GM Place and Gastown. It's well suited to business people, for whom they have set up fax machines, guest-telephone lines and desks in larger rooms. The atmosphere is cozy, the rooms are bright and airy, and you can have your meals on the terrace with a view of the garden.

 The **Westin Bayshore** *($200-$300; bp, tv, ℜ, △, ≈, :P; 1601 W. Georgia St., ☎ 682-3377; ≈ 687-3102)* is a very classy place. Its setting is typically "Vancouver" with the surrounding mountains, the proximity of the sea and the city so close by. The 517 rooms each have their own charm, not to mention the stunning views. Staying here is like staying at a tropical resort.

BURRARD INLET

The **Capilano Bed & Breakfast** *($39-$50 bkfst incl.; tv; 1374 Plateau Dr., ☎ 990-5177, ≈ 990-8889)* is located close to Lions Gate Bridge. Skiers can easily get to Cypress Bowl (15 min) and Grouse Mountain (8 min). Except during rush hour, the hotel is five minutes from Stanley Park, 10 minutes from downtown and Chinatown, and about 25 minutes from the airport. The rooms are attractive, and some have nice views. The complete breakfasts are delicious. Prices for weekly stays can be negotiated and they offer a 20% discount on ski tickets for Grouse Mountain.

The **Globetrotter's Inn** *($40 sb; 45$ pb; tv; 170 West Esplanade, North Vancouver, ☎ 988-2082, ≈ 987-8389)*, in the heart of North Vancouver, near the Seabus and the shops of Marine Drive and the Quay Market, is very affordable.

The **Horseshoe Bay Motel** *($75; tv; 6588 Royal Avenue, West Vancouver, ☎ 921-7454, ≈ 921-7464)*, in the chic neighbourhood of West Vancouver, is advantageously located near the charming little town of Horseshoe Bay and the dock for the ferry to Nanaimo on Vancouver Island.

The **Grouse Inn** *($105; pb, ≡, ≈, tv; 1633 Capilano Rd., North Vancouver, ☎ 988-7101 or 1-800-779-7888, ≈ 988-7102)*, located close to the Grouse Mountain cable car, is great for those who like to be near the mountains.

The **Canyon Court Motel** *($105; tv, ≡, ≈; 1748 Capilano Rd., North Vancouver, ☎ and ≈ 988-3181)* is located right next to the Capilano Suspension Bridge, the Lion's Gate Bridge and the TransCanada Highway. It is very comfortable and not too expensive.

Summit View *($110-$150 bkfst incl.; tv, ℗; 5501 Cliffridge Pl., ☎ 990-1089, ≈ 987-7167)*. To get here from the Lions Gate Bridge, go toward North Vancouver, right on Marine Drive, then, at the first intersection, turn left on Capilano Road, right on Prospect Road, left on Cliffridge Avenue and finally left on Cliffridge Place. To get here from the Second Narrows Bridge, take Highway 1 west and exit onto Capilano Road, then continue as above. Each room has its own character. In the elegant dining room, breakfast and dinner are prepared to order, according to your tastes or diet. Rock-climbing, skiing, fishing, canoeing, swimming and tennis are all possible nearby. The management offers bicycles to help you discover the wonders of the area. Low-season rates are considerably less expensive here.

Palms Guest House *($150-$225 bkfst incl.; pb, tv; 3042 Marine Dr., ☎ 926-1159 or 1-800-691-4455, ≈ 926-1451)*. To get here from Lions Gate Bridge, go left to West Vancouver. Luxurious rooms with a view of the ocean. Easy access to Cypress Bowl and Grouse Mountain ski resorts. Close to the charming little port of Horseshoe Bay, ferries heading to the Sunshine Coast, points of interest in North Vancouver such as Capilano Suspension Bridge and the Capilano Fish Hatchery, and roads leading to Lynn Valley, Mount Seymour and the lovely little bay of Deep Cove.

 The **Lonsdale Quay Hotel** *($200; tv, ≡, ⊚, ☉, ℜ; 123 Carrie Cates Court, North Vancouver, ☎ 986-6111 or 1-800-836-6111, ≈ 986-8782)* is a luxury hotel set magnificently near the shores of Burrard Inlet, above the huge covered Quay Market. The rooms enjoy extraordinary views of downtown Vancouver.

🛏 FALSE CREEK

The **Pillow Porridge Guest House** *($115-$135 bkfst incl.; tv, pb, ℜ, K, ☎; 2859 Manitoba St., ☎ 879-8977, ≈ 897-8966)* is a residence dating back to 1910, and the decor and ambience attest to it. These complete apartments with kitchens are pleasant and comfortable. Close to a number of ethnically diverse restaurants.

Plaza 500 Hotel *($140-$170; pb, tv, ℜ, ≈, ℘; 500 W. 12th Ave., ☎ 873-1811 or 1-800-473-1811)* is just five minutes from the heart of Vancouver and 20 minutes from the airport. Completely renovated, it offers one of the most spectacular views of the mountains and English Bay. Among the best hotels in the city, it offers coffee machines in the rooms and access to the Fitness World club, just across the street.

Chez Phillipe *($175-$225 bkfst incl.; pb, tv, ℜ, K, ℘; by appointment only, ☎ 649-2817)* is located in the heart of Vancouver, in the West End neighbourhood, two steps away from False Creek, in a very holiday-like setting. It's a luxurious apartment on the 17th floor of a modern highrise built at the entrance to the Seawall. To cross False Creek to get to Granville Island Market, you can take a charming little ferry that

ACCOMMODATIONS

leaves from the foot of the building. A generous breakfast is included in the price and you can even cook for yourself if you like. Guests also have access to a dishwasher, a washing machine and a dryer, as well as a full bathroom with a separate shower and a terrace. By reservation only.

 SOUTH VANCOUVER AND SHAUGHNESSY

William House *($95-$190 bkfst incl.; tv, pb, ☎; 2050 W. 18th Ave., ☎ and ≈ 731-2760)* is a beautiful, completely restored country house, in the old area of Shaughnessy, a few minutes from downtown. Luxury suites and rooms offer a pleasantly calm, comfortable environment. The large garden and yard provide havens from all the noise of the city. Well suited to business people. Prices are negotiable depending on the season and the length of your stay.

Stay'n Save Motor Inn *($109; pb, tv, ℘; 1055, St. Edwards Dr., Richmond, 273-3311,☎ 1-800-663-0298, ≈ 273-9522)*. You will recognize it by its blue roof. There are a few in the region; this one is at the airport and offers comfortable surroundings and friendly service. Good mattresses, television with a movie channel included, free local phone calls and attractive decor.

The **Best Western Abercorn Inn** *($140; tv; 9260 Bridgeport Rd., Richmond, ☎ 270-7576 or 1-800-663-0085, ≈ 270-0001)* is relatively affordable for its category. It is located close to the airport and many shopping malls. A good choice for travellers looking for something halfway between the airport and downtown.

Radisson Hotel *(165 $; ≈, ℝ, ℜ, ⊛, ⊙, ⅙, ✗; 8181 Cambie Rd, Richmond; ☎ 276-8181 or 1-800-333-3333, ≈ 279-8381)* is located near the airport and offers a high level of comfort. Rooms have coffee-makers and refrigerators, as well as work desks. Decor in the guest rooms, meeting rooms and restaurants is modern and classic, providing a relaxing atmosphere. A physical fitness centre and pool are well appreciated by some, especially during the rainy season. Next to the hotel is a very impressive Chinese supermarket; the hotel is located in Richmond, a suburb with a high percentage of

Chinese residents. Upstairs from the supermarket is a Buddhist temple where visitors are received gracefully and can have the various aspects of Buddhism explained to them (see "Exploring", p. 104)

The exciting spectacle of planes and seaplanes landing is part of staying at the **Delta Vancouver Airport Hotel and Marina** *($270; tv, ≈, ℜ; 3500 Cessna Drive, Richmond, ☎ 278-1241 or 1-800-268-1133, ≈ 276-1975)*. This hotel offers all the amenities you would expect in a hotel of the Delta chain. It is located on the edge of the airport, close to the Fraser River.

The **Delta Pacific Resort and Conference Centre** *($300; tv, ≈, ℜ, ⅄, ✻; 10251 Saint Edwards Drive, Richmond, ☎ 278-9611 or 1-800-268-1133, ≈ 276-1121)* is a pleasant hotel set amidst the shopping centres of Richmond, a small town about 30 minutes from downtown nicknamed Chinatown II because of its large Chinese community.

THE PENINSULA

Vancouver International Hostel *($16-$20; men's and women's dormitories, some private rooms, sb, tv, cafeteria from Apr to Oct; 151 Discovery St., ☎ 224-3208, ≈ 224-4852)*. Located in Jericho Park, this youth hostel is open day and night; take UBC bus #4 from downtown to reach it. With Locarno and Jericho beaches nearby, this is a great spot for budget travellers.

UBC Housing and Conference Centre *($22-$105; sb or pb, ℂ, ℝ, ℗, ⅄; 5961 Student Union Blvd., ☎ 822-1010, ≈ 822-1001, reservation@brock.housing.ubc.ca)*. In addition to a year-round 48-suite hotel, campus apartments are available from May to August. Inexpensive and well located, near museums, beaches and hiking trails, this spot also provides tranquillity.

 Johnson House Bed & Breakfast *($75-$140 bkfst incl.; sb or pb; Nov-Feb by request only; 2278 West 34th Avenue, Kerrisdale district, ☎ and ≈ 266-4175)* occupies a magnificent, fully renovated house from the 1920s, with an extra floor added. The owners, Sandy and Ron Johnson, carried out the work; they also acquired several of the antiques that form part of the decor.

Penny Farthing Inn Bed & Breakfast *($95-150 bkfst incl.; sb or pb; 2855 West 6th Avenue, Kitsilano, ☎ 739-9002, ⊕ 739-9004, farthing@uniserve.com)*. Lyn Hairstock receives you warmly in her home built in 1912. Wood and stained glass give the four rooms plenty of charm. Smoking not allowed.

RESTAURANTS

This chapter will help you discover all sorts of great little eateries as well as the finest tables in the city, where local specialties as well as international delicacies can be enjoyed.

 GASTOWN

Water Street Café *($; closes at 10pm weekdays, 11pm weekends; 300 Water St., ☎ 689-2832)*. A handsome bistro with big windows facing Gastown. Tables are decorated with pretty lanterns, and service is friendly. The menu centres around pastas prepared in creative ways.

The Old Spaghetti Factory *($; closes about 11pm; 53 Water St., ☎ 684-1288)* is an affordable, quality family restaurant. The turn-of-the-century decor is fun and the service is quick.

Greek Characters *($$; 1 Alexander St., at Maple Tree Sq., ☎ 681-6581)*. Authentic Greek cuisine, moussaka, roasted lamb, souvlaki as well as fish dishes, with a little room left over for French onion soup and Italian pasta dishes.

Top of Vancouver *($$$; Sunday brunch buffet for $26.95; every day 11:30am to 2:30pm and 5pm to 10pm, except Sun*

RESTAURANTS BY TYPE OF CUISINE

brunch at 11am; 555 W. Hastings St., ☎ *669-2220).* This restaurant, located atop Harbour Centre (the elevator is free for restaurant patrons), revolves once an hour, giving diners a city tour from high in the air while they eat. Classic West Coast cuisine is served here.

 # CHINATOWN AND EAST VANCOUVER

RESTAURANTS

Joe's Café *($; 1150 Commercial Dr.).* This spot is frequented by a regular clientele of intellectuals, Sunday philosophers and feminists, among others. What brings them together, most of all, is Joe's coffee.

Waa Zuu Bee Café *($; 1622 Commercial Dr.,* ☎ *253-5299)* is great and inexpensive. The innovative cuisine combined with the "natural-techno-italo-bizarre" decor are full of surprises. The pasta dishes are always interesting.

Nick's Spaghetti House *($-$$; 631 Commercial Dr.,* ☎ *254-5633).* Copious meals are served on red-and-white-checked tablecloths, amidst landscape paintings of Capri and Sorrento. People are friendly here and patrons enter the restaurant through the kitchen, a reassuring element.

Santos Tapas Restaurant *($$; 1191 Commercial Dr.,* ☎ *253-0444).* Latins seem to have a gift for calming the atmosphere with the aromas of their spices and with their music. This is certainly the case here where groups of musicians perform at your table. This restaurant is frequented mostly by Vancouverites.

The **Sun Sui Wah Seafood Restaurant** *($$; every day; 3888 Main St., at 3rd Ave.,* ☎ *872-8822)* was chosen as the "most popular Chinese-food restaurant" in 1996. Authentic Chinese food, lobster, crayfish, crab, oysters and, of course, Peking duck.

The **Cannery Seafood Restaurant** *($$$; until 10:30pm; 2205 Commissioner St.,* ☎ *254-9606)* is one of the best places in town for seafood. It is located in the East End in a renovated century-old warehouse. The view of the sea is fantastic.

 DOWNTOWN

Benny's *($; open 24 hours a day; 2505 W. Broadway, ☎ 731-9730)* has a funky, relaxed decor.

A relaxing ambience and family-style fare are served up at the **Dining Car** *($; Mon to Fri noon to 2:30pm, Fri and Sat 5pm to 10pm; at the Railway Club, 579 Dunsmuir St., ☎ 681-1625)*, where the clientele runs the gamut from suits to artists.

India Gate *($; 616 Robson St., ☎ 684-4617)*. You can get a curry dish for as little as $5.95 at lunchtime. In the evening, this restaurant is rather deserted. The decor is not at all exotic.

Malone's Bar & Grill *($; every day; 608 W. Pender St., ☎ 684-9977)*. You can enjoy steak, salmon, chicken, pizza or beer, all reasonably priced, while watching a hockey game on their giant screen. Music and Cuban cigars.

The **Arena Ristorante** *($$; 300 W. Georgia St., ☎ 687-5434)* serves Italian specialties. The atmosphere is livelier on Friday and Saturday nights when they present live jazz performances.

Chateau Madrid - La Bodega *($$; closed Sun and holidays; 277 Howe St., ☎ 684-8814)*. Restaurant and tapas bar; traditional paella and sangria.

The **Hard Rock Café** *($$; until 1am; 686 W. Hastings St., ☎ 687-ROCK)* is part of the famous worldwide chain of restaurants where paraphernalia from famous rock stars and Harley Davidson gadgets decorate the walls, and delicious burgers and nachos are served.

The **Monterey Grill** *($$; 1277 Robson St., ☎ 688-0461)* serves breakfasts, mixed dishes, organic salads and chicken in a pleasant and tasteful setting. Live jazz on Thursdays, Fridays and Saturdays; large windows opening out onto a terrace overlooking Robson Street.

Planet Hollywood *($$; every day; 969 Robson St., ☎ 688-7827)*. The theme of the decor is television and film. They show movies and a lot of advertising on giant screens and offer a simple menu: burgers, fries and drinks. T-shirts and gadgets are for sale in the boutique. Worth investigating only if you've never been to a Planet Hollywood.

Settebello *($$; 1133 Robson St., ☎ 681-7377)*. Pizzas and salads with olive oil and Italian bread; warm ambiance; lovely dining room and a terrace decorated with flowers.

Tsunami Sushi *($$; 238-1025 Robson St., ☎ 687-8744)* has a revolving sushi bar, much like those in Japan, from which patrons can choose specialties at will. Excellent quality for the price; huge, sunny terrace overlooking Robson Street.

The **Yaletown Brewing Co.** *($$; closed midnight; 1111 Mainland St., ☎ 681-2739)* is a veritable yuppie temple in the post-industrial neighbourhood of Yaletown and a fun place to spend an evening. Try the pizza from the wood-burning oven.

🦐 **Joe Fortes** *($$$; 777 Thurlow St., at Robson, ☎ 669-1940)* is renowned in the West End for its oysters and other seafood. This bistro, with it's turn-of-the-century decor and heated upstairs terrace, has an appetizing menu. This is a popular meeting place for successful young professionals.

🦐 **Le Crocodile** *($$$-$$$$; 909 Burrard St., entry by Smithe St., ☎ 669-4298)*. This establishment is the beacon of French cuisine in Vancouver, as much for the quality of its food as for its service, its decor and its wine list. Lovers of great French cuisine will be spoiled by the choice of red meats and the delicacies from the sea. The salmon tartare is a must, you *are* on the Pacific coast after all!

Lumière *($$$$; 2551 W. Boradway Ave., ☎ 739-8185)* is a favourite with Vancouver residents, especially chefs. The simple, white interior allows the food the shine, and shine it does. The fresh, local ingredients used in each dish make for creative and honest, but very refined, fusion cuisine. One winning choice is veal tenderloin with braised turnip lasagna topped off by lemon tarts or chocolate truffles.

THE WEST END

The **Bagel Street Café** *($; 1218 Robson St., ☎ 688-6063)* makes all kinds of bagels for all tastes. Lettuce and cheese are the predominant trimmings. A variety of coffees and teas are also available.

Bino's restaurants *($; 885 W. Broadway, ☎ 874-7415; 2126 W. Broadway, ☎ 733-6316; 2001 Lonsdale Ave., North Vancouver, ☎ 985-4516)* serve crepes and Canadian cuisine.

Bread Garden *($; 24 hours a day; three locations in the same area: 1040 Denman St., ☎ 685-2996; 812 Bute St., ☎ 688-3213; 2996 Granville St., ☎ 736-6465)*. These cafés sell bread, pastries and tasty prepared dishes to go, such as quiches, lasagnas, sandwiches, and fruit plates. Good vegetarian selections. You can also enjoy all of these in-house. Good service and low prices. Also located at 1880 West 1st Avenue, Kitsilano, ☎ 738-6684; 550 Park Royal North, West Vancouver, ☎ 925-0181; 4575 Central Boulevard, Burnaby, ☎ 435-5177.

Ciao Espresso Bar *($; 1074 Denman St., ☎ 682-0112)*. Folks come to this little West End establishment for the strong, dark brew and the neighbourhood atmosphere.

At **La Crêpe Bretonne** *($; 795 Jervis St., ☎ 608-1266)*, you can enjoy a large variety of crepes – with sugar, eggs, ham or chicken – all to the sound of French songs hummed by the owner. Worth a visit.

Da Pasta Bar *($; 1232 Robson St., ☎ 688-1288)*. This Italian restaurant, located in the most refined part of Robson Street, offers original items such as pasta with curry. Full lunches for $7.50. Pleasant decor.

The **DV8** *($; 525 Davie St., ☎ 682-4388)* is a café.

Flying Wedge Pizza Co. *($; Royal Centre, 1055 W. Georgia St., ☎ 681-1233; 3499 Cambie St., ☎ 874-8284; 1937 Cornwall, Kitsilano, ☎ 732-8840; Vancouver Airport, ☎ 303-3370; Library Square, ☎ 689-7078)*. Pizza lovers, these are addresses to jot down if you're looking for pizza that doesn't remind you of something you ate last week. You'll get a discount if you bring your own plate, showing that you're ecologically minded.

The **Fresgo Inn Restaurant & Bakery** *($; 1138 Davie St.,* ☎ *689-1332)* is fairly renowned for its portions and prices.

The **Kitto Japanese House** *($; until midnight, Fri and Sat 1am, 833 Bute St.,* ☎ *662-3333)* is the local teriyaki specialist, with inexpensive, quality dishes. Service is quick and the staff are friendly.

Luxy Bistro *($; 1235 Davie St.,* ☎ *681-9976)*. The menu of this little, dark-green-walled restaurant offers pasta dishes prepared with all sorts of ingredients and just as much imagination. Good quality and reasonable prices. People come for the atmosphere more than anything, especially on weekend evenings.

Starbucks *($; 1099 Robson St.,* ☎ *685-1099)*. A green logo marks the spot. Capuccino, espresso, big, small, medium, strong, weak, decaf, with milk, cold with chocolate or nutmeg: the choice is yours. Charming terrace. Several other branches of this Seattle-based chain are scattered around Vancouver and surrounding areas.

True Confections *($; until 1am; 866 Denman St.,* ☎ *682-1292)* is a dessert place par excellence with huge slices of cake. Be sure to try the divine Belgian dark-chocolate torte.

Kamei Sushi *($-$$; 1414 W. Broadway,* ☎ *732-0112)*. This chain of Japanese restaurants offers excellent dishes at reasonable prices. Service is efficient and pleasant. A fine Asian experience.

Sakae Japanese Restaurant *($-$$ for lunch; 745 Thurlow St.,* ☎ *669-0067)*. It is easy to walk right past this restaurant, situated in the basement of a commercial building, but the welcoming smiles and the quality of the food compensate for its location. The sushi and sashimi will literally melt in your mouth.

Cocorico's *($$; at Robson and Jervis)*. Either inside or outside, a pleasant spot to sample good French pastries, sandwiches or soup, with a fine coffee, a beer or a glass of wine.

RESTAURANTS

Gyoza King *($$; 1508 Robson St., ☎ 669-8278)*. The items served here range from teriyaki dishes to sashimi and include the chef's specialties such as marinated anchovies. Warm atmosphere.

Liliget *($$; every day; 1724 Davie St., ☎ 681-7044)* is a First Nations restaurant. It offers authentic native food: salmon grilled on a wood fire, smoked oysters, grilled seaweed, roasted wild duck. Worth exploring.

Marbella *($$; 1368 Robson St., ☎ 681-1175)* is a Spanish restaurant mostly frequented by tourists. They serve excellent garlic shrimp with *margaritas*, various salads, tapas and, notably, real paella. Spanish guitarists and dancers on Thursdays and Fridays.

The Latin-American and Mexican cuisine of **Mescallero** *($$; until midnight weekdays, 1am weekends; 1215 Bidwell St., ☎ 669-2399)* is served in a pretty setting with a friendly ambience; things get really busy on Saturday evenings.

Miko Sushi *($$; Mon to Sat; 1335 Robson St., ☎ 681-0339)*. Meticulously prepared Japanese food; extremely fresh sushi and sashimi; impeccable service in this small restaurant. Reservations recommended.

Milestone's *($$; 1210 Denman St., ☎ 662-3431)*. The hamburger plates, steaks and salads come in generous portions. Freshly-squeezed fruit juices. Lovely terrace facing English Bay.

Raku *($$; 838 Thurlow St., north of Robson, ☎ 685-8817)* A wealthy young Japanese clientele meets here and fits right in. It has the atmosphere of a noisy bar, but it is an ideal spot to begin a promising evening. The sushi and grilled meats are recommended.

The Italian restaurant **Romano's Macaroni Grill** *($$; until 10pm, 11pm weekends, 1523 Davie, ☎ 689-4334)* is located in an enormous mansion. Fine olive oil on each table is just part of the cosy atmosphere. Children (and adults too) can draw on the tables with crayons provided by the restaurant. Go on a Sunday for the all-you-can-eat pasta brunch.

Yiannis *($$; 1642 Robson St., ☎ 681-8141)* has red walls on the outside and lovely blue-and-white decor on the inside with skylights. The selection of small cold appetizers is varied, and combination plates aren't very expensive. The souvlakis and roasted lamb are delicious. Good service, pleasant atmosphere

C *($$$; 1600 Howe St., ☎ 605-8263)*. This Chinese restaurant, whose name evokes the sea, has just opened in Vancouver. It is already provoking much talk, and with good reason. The chef has returned from Southeast Asia with innovative and unique recipes. Served on the stroke of twelve, the *C*-style Dim Sum is a real delight. Titbits of fish marinated in tea and a touch of caviar, vol-au-vents with chanterelles, curry shrimp with coconut milk, and the list goes on... All quite simply exquisite. Desserts are equally extraordinary. For those who dare, the crème brûlée with blue cheese is an unforgettable experience. This restaurant is an absolute must.

The **Raincity Grill** *($$$; until 10:30pm; 1193 Denman St., ☎ 685-7337)* specializes in grilled fish and meats in true West Coast tradition. A bit pricey.

L'Hermitage *($$$-$$$$; every day; 115-1025 Robson St., ☎ 689-3237)*. The chef-owner Hervé Martin, is an artist when it comes to French cuisine and will tell you stories from his days as the chef of the Belgian Royal Court. Wines from his native region of Burgundy accompany the finest of dishes, each prepared carefully and with panache. The decor is chic and the service exemplary. The terrace, set back from Robson, is lovely in the summertime.

The **Cloud 9 Revolving Restaurant** *($$$$; until 11pm; 1400 Robson St., ☎ 687-0511)* is an experience. This resto-bar at the top of the 40-story Landmark hotel offers an exceptional view. It takes 80 minutes for the restaurant to turn 360°. Sunset is particularly picturesque as the sky darkens and the city begins to glow. Try the lamb chops or the salmon.

Le Gavroche *($$$$; evenings every day and mornings Mon to Fri; 1616 Alberni St., ☎ 685-3924)*. Fine French cuisine in a Victorian house. Reservations required.

RESTAURANTS

STANLEY PARK

The Prospect Point Café *($; Stanley Park, ☎ 669-2737)* is located at the historical observation site on the tip of Stanley Park. You can contemplate Lions Gate Bridge at sunset and sample steaks, pasta and chicken burgers.

The **Fish House in Stanley Park** *($$$; until 10:30pm; 8901 Stanley Park Dr., ☎ 681-7275)* is located in a Victorian house right in the heart of the park and just a few steps from the Seawall. Fine seafood and fish dishes are served in an opulent and lovely decor.

The **Teahouse Restaurant** *($$$; until 10pm, along the Seawall, ☎ 669-3281)* serves delicious food and affords stunning views of English Bay from Stanley Park. Call ahead for reservations and for precise directions as it can be tricky to find.

 BURRARD INLET

Bean Around the World *($; 1522 Marine Dr., West Vancouver, ☎ 925-9600)*. A crowd of rather laid-back people squeezes into this warm spot. Excellent coffees and sweets are served at reasonable prices.

The **Beach Side Café** *($$; 1362 Marine Dr., ☎ 925-1945)*, in West Vancouver, is a lovely restaurant with original recipes prepared from local produce, as well as meat and fish dishes.

The **Boathouse** *($$; until 9:30pm, 10pm weekends; 6995 Nelson Ave., Horseshoe Bay, ☎ 921-8188)* is a large glassed-in restaurant at the heart of the quaint community of Horseshoe Bay. Seafood is its specialty: oysters, halibut, salmon...

Bridge House Restaurant *($$; summer every day, winter Wed to Sun; Sun brunch 11am to 2pm; 3650 Capilano Rd., North Vancouver, ☎ 987-3388)*. In a warm and intimate, English-style setting, this restaurant serves traditional Canadian dishes, homemade pies and warm bread. Reservations recommended.

Imperial *($$-$$$$; Mon to Fri 11am to 2:30pm and 5pm to 10pm, Sat and Sun and holidays 10:30am to 2:30pm and 5pm to 10pm; 355 Burrard St., ☎ 688-8191).* Located in the Marine Building, an Art Deco architectural masterpiece (see p 76), this Chinese restaurant also has several Art Deco elements, but it is the big windows looking over Burrard Inlet that are especially fascinating. In this very elegant spot, boys in livery and discreet young ladies perform the *dim sum* ritual. Unlike elsewhere, there are no carts here: the various steamed dishes are brought on trays. You can also ask for a list, allowing you to choose your favourites among the 30 or so on offer. The quality of the food matches the excellent reputation this restaurant has acquired.

The Salmon House *($$$; every day; 2229 Folkestone Way, West Vancouver, ☎ 926-8539)* offers unique, creative cuisine that focuses on salmon in a superb, Canadian-cedar decor. A view of the ocean, the city and Stanley Park adds to the pleasure of the palate.

 FALSE CREEK

La Baguette et L'Échalotte *($; 1680 Johnston St., ☎ 684-1351).* If you expect to be picnicking during your visit to Granville Island, here is where you will find French bread, pastries, croissants and take-out dishes. Louise and Mario take good care of this little shop, located in the heart of busy Granville Island.

The **Bridges Bistro** *($; until 11:30pm; 1696 Durenleau St., Granville Island, ☎ 687-4400, ≈ 687-0352)* boasts one of the prettiest terraces in Vancouver, right by the water in the middle of Granville Island's pleasure-boat harbour. The food and setting are decidedly West Coast.

De Dutch Pannekoek House *($; 2622 Granville St., ☎ 731-0775)* is a specialist in pancake breakfasts. Big beautiful pancakes are made to order, plain or with your favourite fillings. There are about ten of these restaurants, including one at 1725 Robson Street and another at 1260 Davie. The one on Granville is calm and pleasant, and the service is perfect.

RESTAURANTS

Kamei Royale Ocean *($$; 1333 Johnston St., Granville Island,* ☎ *602-0005)* is a conveniently located and lovely restaurant. Sushi, sashimi, *miso* and teriyaki are the house specialties. It offers a wonderful view overlooking the cove. Fast service.

Meat-eaters converge on **The Keg** *($$; until 10pm, midnight weekends; 1499 Anderson St., Granville Island,* ☎ *685-4735).* There are lots of steaks to choose from and prices are reasonable. The atmosphere is relaxed and the staff particularly friendly.

Monk McQueens *($$; every day; 601 Stamps Landing,* ☎ *877-1351).* Specialties are fish and an oyster buffet. This restaurant overlooks the inlet and has the decor of a small sailing club. Very pleasant inside and on the terrace. Impeccable service and delicious food. A pianist accompanies your meal.

The **Royal Seoul House Korean Restaurant** *($$; 1215 W. Broadway,* ☎ *738-8285 or 739-9001)* has a large dining room divided into compartments. Each compartment has a table with a grill for preparing food and can accommodate four or more people. Order your all-you-can-eat meat, fish and seafood buffet, and have fun. Everything here is good, including the service.

Seasons in the Park *($$$-$$$$; right in Queen Elizabeth Park, 33 Cambie St.,* ☎ *874-8008)* is a pleasant restaurant with classic, elegant decor and an unhindered view of the city. Succulent cuisine. Reservations required.

SOUTH VANCOUVER AND SHAUGHNESSY

The **Big News Coffee Bar** *($; 2447 Granville St., at Broadway,* ☎ *739-7320)*, an alternative to Starbucks, is a pleasant neighbourhood café. The decor is modern and sober and they offer fast service, good coffee and a number of magazines and newspapers to leaf through while you eat.

THE PENINSULA

Combo Restaurant *($; 2525 Heather St., ☎ 876-6989)* features Chinese food.

The **Funky Armadillo Café** *($; until midnight, 1am weekends; 2741 W. 4th Ave., ☎ 739-8131)*, with its modern, unpretentious, quality food, is considered the cocktail specialist of Vancouver. Frequented by a socially aware clientele.

The Naam *($; 2724 W. 4th Ave., ☎ 738-7151, open 24 hours)* blends live music with vegetarian meals. This little restaurant has a warm atmosphere and friendly service. This spot is frequented by a young clientele.

Sophie's Cosmic Café *($; 2095 W. 4th Ave., ☎ 732-6810)*. This is a weekend meeting-spot for the Kitsilano crowd, who come to stuff themselves with bacon and eggs. 1950s decor, relaxed atmosphere.

The Vineyard *($; 2296 W. 4th Ave., ☎ 733-2420)* serves Greek specialties.

Japanese Bistro Kitsilano *($$; 1815 W. 1st Ave., ☎ 734-5858)* features an all-you-can-eat sushi and tempura buffet. Large terrace; excellent service.

Las Margaritas *($$; until 10pm, 11pm weekends; 1999 W. 4th Ave., ☎ 734-7117)* serves healthy Mexican fare in a lively setting with lots of ambience. A great place to go with a group of friends.

Mark's Steak and Tap House *($$; until 1:30am; 2486 Bayswater St., ☎ 734-1325)* is a yuppie hangout on the West Side whose parking lot is filled with Harleys on a regular basis. The food is Italian with pastas, pizzas, and the mood is relaxed with jazz in the evenings.

Peppitas Tapa Bar and Grill *($$; 2505 Alma St., ☎ 222-2244)*. Lovers of jazz trios and of excellent desserts have no hesitation in coming here. Kitsilano's young professionals frequent this spot, which is a bit expensive.

RESTAURANTS

Sonona on 4th *($$; 1688 W. 4th Ave., ☎ 738-8777)* is like three restaurants in one: it serves West Coast, Asian and Australian cuisines. The atmosphere is very mellow and the desserts are delicious.

Raku Kushiyaki Restaurant *($$-$$$; 4422 W. 10th Ave., ☎ 222-8188)*. The young chefs of this little restaurant prepare local cuisine served with oriental aesthetic rules in mind; they will help you discover their art. Take a meal for two to appreciate the spirit of this *nouvelle cuisine*, which encourages the sharing of meals among guests. The portions may seem small, but you still come away satiated. Ingredients are chosen according to the seasons, for example wild mushrooms are served accented with garlic, green bell peppers, butter, soya sauce and lime juice. This dish may seem simple, and it is, but the taste of the food is not masked by some mediocre sauce. The meats and fish are also treated with subtlety.

Star Anise *($$$$; every day 5:30pm to 11pm, and Mon to Fri 11:30am to 2pm; 1485 W. 12th Ave., ☎ 737-1485)* is a very pretty and stylish restaurant frequented by the beautiful people. Big paintings adorn the yellow walls, and lanterns illuminate the tables.

ENTERTAINMENT

 ARTS Hotline *(☎ 684-ARTS)* will inform you about all shows (dance, theatre, music, cinema and literature) in the city.

Ticketmaster: ☎ 280-4444

Arts Line: ☎ 280-3311 (for tickets only)

Sports Line: ☎ 280-4400

For information on jazz shows in Vancouver, call the **Jazz Hotline** *(☎ 682-0706)*.

The Georgia Straight (☎ 730-7000). This weekly paper is published every Thursday and distributed free at many spots in Vancouver. You will find all the necessary information on coming shows and cultural events. This paper is read religiously each week by many Vancouverites and has acquired a good reputation.

BARS AND NIGHTCLUBS

Gastown

The **Blarney Stone** *(216 Carrall St.)* is the spot for authentic Irish jigs and reels. The ambience is frenetic with people dancing everywhere, on the tables, on the chairs... A must-see!

Lamplighter's Bar *(210 Abbott St., ☎ 681-6666)*. A diverse assortment of people frequent this unpretentious bar. Local blues bands play here.

The Purple Onion Cabaret *(every day; 15 Water St., 3rd floor, ☎ 602-9442)* is the mecca of upbeat jazz in Vancouver, with entertainment provided by a disc-jockey or live bands. Cover charge of three dollars during the week and seven dollars on weekends. Wednesdays are dedicated to Latin jazz; on Fridays and Saturdays there's live jazz near the bar and "disco-funk" on the dance floor.

Sonar *(66 Water St., ☎ 683-6695)*. Alternative and underground DJ format with some live shows on this Gastown stage. The place is very big, and you can play pool.

Chinatown and East Vancouver

The Hot Jazz Society *(2120 Main St., ☎ 873-4131)* was one of the first places in Vancouver to offer good jazz. It's a veritable institution where many of the big names in jazz perform. Call to find out who's playing.

If you're feeling lucky, try your hand at the **Royal Diamond Casino** *(750 Pacific Blvd. S., ☎ 685-2340)*. Casinos in British Columbia are government owned and all the winnings are donated to charity. A good system!

Downtown

Athletic Billiards Café *(1011 Hamilton St., ☎ 669-3533)*. Hip, young atmosphere; good pool tables. Located downtown, at the edge of Yaletown.

Automotive Billiards Club *(1095 Homer St., ☎ 682-0040)*. Very good music, excellent pool tables and great expresso. They also serve sandwiches. There's a small divider separating the pool-table area from the bar corner. Also, it's one of the rare pool halls to serve beer. Hip, friendly atmosphere on weekends.

ENTERTAINMENT

Babalu *(654 Nelson St., at Granville St., ☎ 605-4343)* is a brand new lounge-style bar. It's the ideal spot to sip a cocktail while enjoying a little Frank Sinatra and a cigar. There is also dancing to jazzy rhythms. Cover charge of three dollars.

Bar None *(1222 Hamilton St., ☎ 689-7000)* is the hang-out of Vancouver's trendy youth. A friendly pub atmosphere is complemented by a dance floor. Watch out for long line-ups on Friday and Saturday evenings.

Casbah Jazzbah *(175 W. Pender St., ☎ 669-0837)*. With its choice of performers, this bar-restaurant is currently establishing a solid reputation in the Vancouver jazz scene. It's located on the eastern edge of downtown. One important detail: the neighbourhood isn't very safe at night. Don't park too far away.

Chameleon Urban Lounge *(every day; 801 W. Georgia St., ☎ 669-0806)*. This excellent little downtown club is often packed on weekends unfortunately, but it is calm during the week. Don't miss their trip-hop nights on Wednesdays, Afro-Cuban and latin music on Thursdays, and Acid Jazz on Saturdays. Warning: get there early to avoid lineups. The cover charge is five dollars on Fridays and Saturdays.

The Gate *(1176 Granville St., ☎ 608-4283)*, a jeans-and-beer kind of bar, is open seven days a week and is best known for its lively rock shows. The best nights are from Thursday to Saturday, and the cover charge varies depending on the bands.

Graceland *(Mon to Sat; 1250 Richards St., ☎ 688-2648)* is a club for young techno fans. Saturdays are definitely the most representative of what this dark, psychedelically lit bar has to offer. Cover charge: six dollars on Fridays and Saturdays.

Level 5 *(Thu to Sun; 595 Hornby St., ☎ 602-0051)*, located a few minutes away by foot from the main downtown hotels, hosts a wide variety of performances. Saturdays are devoted to rhythm & blues and funk.

For a heady night of techno and alternative music and dancing, check out **Luv-a-Fair** *(1275 Seymour St., ☎ 685-3288)*. Young crowd.

Madison's Nightspot *(Wed to Sat; 398 Richards St.,* ☎ *687-5007)* is a club that is mostly frequented by young, well-off people, the majority of them of Chinese origin. Cover charge is from three to five dollars. They have "Funky Fridays" and R&B and funk on Saturdays.

Mardi Gras *(1015 Burrard St.,* ☎ *687-0575)* is a club connected to the Century Plaza Hotel catering mostly to tourists during the summer. Mature clientele and very pleasant atmosphere on weekends. Good dance music.

Mars *(Tue to Sat; 1320 Richards St.,* ☎ *662-7707)* is a large bar with a somewhat "showy" clientele, mostly consisting of young, rich Asians. Cover charge: up to eight dollars. On Thursdays they have a good Mecca Hip Hop and R&B night. The Mars restaurant serves West-Coast dishes.

The best night at the **Piccadilly Pub** *(620 W. Pender St.,* ☎ *682-3221)* is Thursday, when groovy funk and acid-jazz make up the line-up.

Railway Club *(admission charged; 579 Dunsmuir St.,* ☎ *681-1625)*. Folk music or blues are presented in an oblong spot that brings to mind a railway car. A miniature electric train runs in a loop above customers' heads as they enjoy the live music.

Richard's on Richards *(1036 Richard St.,* ☎ *687-6794)* is an institution in Vancouver. People of all ages flock to this chic spot to see and be seen. Theme nights. A must try.

The Roxy *(every day; 932 Granville St.,* ☎ *331-7999)* is a boisterous rock club where the beer flows abundantly. Regulars include young professionals and a few cowboys. Cruising appears to be one of the favourite pastimes here. Cover charge: seven dollars.

Royal Hotel *(1025 Granville St.,* ☎ *685-5335)*. A gay crowd throngs to a "modern" decor. Friday evenings are very popular, perhaps because of the live music. People wait in line as early as 5:30pm, though Sunday evenings are more worth it.

The Shark Club *(Mon to Sat; 180 W. Georgia St.,* ☎ *687-4275)* is a modern bar with televisions hanging from the ceiling beaming out hockey or football games. Draught beer is the beverage of choice and baseball hats are the standard clothing accessory. Cover charge: four dollars.

Soho Café & Billiards *(688-1144 Homer St.,* ☎ *688-1180)*, one block away from the Automotive Billiards Club, is very inviting with its cozy wood and brick decor. The pool tables are in the basement.

The **Starfish Room** *(Mon to Sat; 1055 Homer St.,* ☎ *682-4171)* is a good place to hear often very talented live bands of various styles. Check out their ad in the *Georgia Straight* for details.

The **Stone Temple Cabaret** *(1082 Granville St.,* ☎ *488-1333)* is a new bar in a not-too-safe part of town, with Greek columns at the entrance. Dance music on Saturdays and disco on Tuesdays.

Yale Hotel *(1300 Granville St.,* ☎ *681-9253)*. The big names in blues regularly play at this, the blues Mecca of Vancouver. Great ambience on the weekends. The cover charge varies depending on the performers.

The **Yaletown Brewing Co.** *(1111 Mainland St.,* ☎ *681-2739)* is a popular yuppie hangout in Yaletown. The ideal spot for an evening with some friends and some brews.

West End

Barclay Lounge *(1348 Robson St.,* ☎ *688-8850)* is a cabaret-style bar connected to O'Doul's restaurant. The atmosphere is lush and the acts are talented. It's the perfect place to sip a scotch and listen to songs originally performed by Billie Holiday or Sidney Bechet.

Jolting Fish Billiards *(201-1323 Robson St.,* ☎ *685-8015)*. This modern, colourful bar is smoke-free. Located on the second floor with an unobstructed view of Robson Street and two steps away from the major downtown hotels. Young, relaxed atmosphere.

Our Place Billiards *(1046 Davie St., ☎ 682-8368)* is a small room with a few tables. Regular clientele, inexpensive and friendly.

False Creek

The **Big Bam Boo Club** *($5; Wed to Sun; 1236 W. Broadway, ☎ 733-2220)* would be classified as a "strut and cruise" bar, also known for its Ladies Nights on Wednesdays and Saturdays with male strippers. It's definitely a pick-up joint *par excellence*.

Blue Note Jazz Bistro *(2340 W. 4th Ave., ☎ 733-0330)*. Very lively from Thursday night on, this restaurant offers very good "jazz-dining". Worth visiting.

The Fairview Pub *(898 W. Broadway St., ☎ 872-1262)*. Good blues in a friendly atmosphere. Outside the downtown area. Be prepared to line up on weekends.

The Rage *(750 Pacific Blvd. S., ☎ 685-5585)* is another good bar for live music. They play all styles but it's predominantly rock. Refer to the ad in the *Georgia Straight* for all the details. Open on Fridays *($5)* and Saturdays *($7)*.

Yuk Yuk's *(Plaza of Nations, ☎ 687-5233)* is Vancouver's famous comedy club. Varied programme; phone for details.

South Vancouver and Shaughnessy

Lafflines Comedy Club *(26 4th St., New Westminster, ☎ 525-2262)*. Located in the southeast suburbs of Vancouver, this comedy club presents local comedians. Call for details.

Gay and Lesbian Bars

Celebrities *(free admission; 1022 Davie St., ☎ 689-3180)* is definitely the best-known gay bar in Vancouver. Straights also come here for the music. Drag queens make conspicuous appearances, especially on Wednesdays, during the Female Impersonators night. Packed on weekends.

ENTERTAINMENT

Charlie's Lounge *(455 Abbott St., ☎ 685-7777)* is a relaxed bar with an elegant gay clientele, located on the ground floor of an old hotel. Opens at 4pm on Mondays and Tuesdays and at 3pm from Wednesday to Saturday. Sundays, they serve brunch from 11am to 2pm. Musical improv sessions in the afternoon and retro dance music at night.

Chuck's Pub *(every day 11am to 1am; 455 Abbott St., ☎ 685-7777)*. In the same hotel as Charlie's Lounge, with an equally relaxed and elegant atmosphere. Pub style. The Black Apple - Leather/Levis on Saturday nights.

Denman Station *(free admission; 860 Denman St., ☎ 669-3448)* is a small, basement bar with a regular clientele. Thursdays are Electro Lush Lounge nights; Fridays, High Energy Dance Music; Saturdays, Miss Willie Taylor's All Star Show at 11pm; Sundays, karaoke.

The **Lotus Club** *(455 Abbott St., ☎ 685-7777)* is the only bar in Vancouver reserved exclusively for women. It's located in the same hotel as Charlie's Lounge and Chuck's Pub, on the ground floor.

Numbers Cabaret *(1098 Davie St., ☎ 685-4077)*. Located two steps away from Celebrities, this large cabaret is mostly frequented by gay men of all ages.

The **Odyssey** *($2-$4; every day; Howe St., ☎ 689-5256)* is a gay bar where young people go to meet in a fun-loving atmosphere. GoGo Boys-Homo Homer nights on Fridays and Saturdays. Drag queens on Wednesdays and Sundays, with Feather Boa nights starting at 10pm.

 CULTURAL ACTIVITIES AND FESTIVALS

Theatres

Art's Club Theatre *(1585 Johnston, ☎ 687-1644)* is a steadfast institution on the Vancouver theatre scene. Located on the waterfront on Granville Island, this theatre presents contemporary works with social themes. Audience members often get together in the theatre's bar after the plays.

Bard on the Beach *(Vanier Park, ☎ 737-0625 or 739-0559)* is an annual event in honour of Shakespeare. Plays are presented, all in costumes from the era, under a huge tent on a peninsula with a view of English Bay. Goes from mid-June to the end of September.

The **Carousel Theatre Company** *(1405 Anderson, ☎ 669-3410)* is also on Granville Island. It's a small well-established theatre company with a school.

The **Centennial Theatre Centre** *(2300 Lonsdale Ave., North Vancouver, ☎ 984-4484)* is an excellent neighbourhood theatre located in North Vancouver. The auditorium seats over 700 people and has very good acoustics. All types of shows are presented here.

The **Firehall Arts Centre** *(280 E. Cordova St., ☎ 689-0926)*, in the east-central part of the city, has a very good reputation and, like Art's Club Theatre, presents contemporary plays dealing with social themes. Worth a visit.

The **Ford Centre for the Performing Arts** *(777 Homer St., ☎ 280-2222)* is an immense, big-budget theatre that presents international mega-productions like *Show Boat*, *Les Misérables* and *The Phantom of the Opera*.

The **Green Thumb Theatre for Young People** *(1885 Venables St., ☎ 254-4055)* is a small theatre troupe that puts on plays for children. The theatre is in the east end of the city, close to the Vancouver East Cultural Centre.

The **Orpheum Theatre** *(Smithe St., at Seymour St., ☎ 665-3050)*, dating back to the beginning of the century, doesn't look like much from the outside, but on the inside the rococo decor is a pleasant surprise. Most of the presentations here are musical; the Vancouver Symphonic Orchestra performs here regularly.

Performance Works *(1218 Cartwright, ☎ 666-8139)* is another theatre presenting contemporary plays: similar repertoire to the Firehall Arts Centre and Art's Club Theatre.

ENTERTAINMENT

The **Queen Elizabeth Theatre** *(Hamilton St., at Georgia St.,* ☎ *665-3050)*, a large hall with 2,000 seats, presents musicals and variety shows, but is also the main performance space for the Vancouver Opera.

The **Station St. Art Centre** *(930 Station St.,* ☎ *688-3312)* is located in a seedy part of the city, one block east of Main Street. The plays range in nature from experimental to classical, touching on the contemporary.

Le Studio 16 *(1545 W. 7th Ave.,* ☎ *736-1621)*, a multi-purpose hall, is part of the *Maison de la Francophonie de Vancouver*. It is primarily used for Francophone activities, although Anglophone productions are also presented quite often. Le Studio 16 is home to British Columbia's only Francophone theatre troupe: *Le Théâtre La Seizième*. Call for information on upcoming shows. Take note that the troupe is often away on tour.

Vancouver East Cultural Centre *(1895 Venables St.,* ☎ *254-9578)*. "The Cult" is an arts centre which has built a solid reputation over the years for the quality of the shows presented. Theatre, comedy, singing and jazz: it all takes place in this cozy, dimly-lit performance space. A great experience.

Vancouver Opera *(845 Cambie St.,* ☎ *682-2871)*. Vancouver is one of the major cities in the world that doesn't have an opera house. For this reason, all operas are presented at the Queen Elizabeth Theatre, at Hamilton and Georgia Streets. The address here is for the administration office where you can phone for program information.

The **Vancouver Playhouse Theatre** *(Hamilton St. at Dunsmuir St.,* ☎ *873-3311)* is another multidisciplinary performance space offering concerts, musicals and plays. The shows are always of high calibre. Worth investigating.

The old **Vogue Theatre** *(918 Granville,* ☎ *331-7900)*, renovated not long ago, follows the trend in Vancouver of being able to present all types of shows: theatre, comedy, music and even film. The programming varies. Call for details.

The Waterfront Theatre *(1410 Cartwright,* ☎ *685-6217)* is an ultramodern performance space that also serves multiple functions. Located at the entrance to Granville Island, the Waterfront presents both theatre and concerts. Check the programming and performance times in the *Georgia Straight* or by calling.

Movie Theatres

Capitol 6 *(820 Granville St., ☎ 669-6000)*. Large downtown theatre showing the latest Hollywood productions. Dolby digital sound.

Caprice *(965 Granville St., ☎ 683-6099)*. The only theatre decorated in Las Vegas style with sequined curtains. They show art and repertory films, as well as quality foreign films.

The **CN IMAX Cinema** *(2nd floor, Canada Place, ☎ 682-IMAX)* consists of a seven-story-high screen and digital, 2,000-watt sound. The IMAX system is an extraordinary audiovisual experience. Call for the schedule of 3-D films being presented.

The **Granville 7** *(855 Granville St., ☎ 684-4000)* is located right across from the Capitol 6 and is also a large theatre showing the latest Hollywood productions. DDSS-THX sound.

The **Hollywood** *(3123 W. Broadway, ☎ 738-3211)* is a small neighbourhood theatre (Kitsilano) that shows second-run films at reasonable prices (under $4).

The **Pacific Cinematheque** *(1131 Howe St., ☎ 688-8202)* is *the* place to go for film buffs. Information on their extensive programming is available at the Cinematheque or by phone.

The **Park Theatre** *(3440 Cambie St., ☎ 290-0500)* is a repertory theatre that always shows enticing films. It's located in a pleasant part of town.

The **Ridge Theatre** *(3131 Arbutus St., ☎ 738-6311)*, is another repertory theatre, located in the west end of the city. They always offer interesting films, including good-quality recent releases and foreign classics.

ENTERTAINMENT

Vancouver Centre Cinemas *(650 W. Georgia St.,* ☎ *669-4442)*. The latest Hollywood productions presented in modern theatres with digital sound.

The **Varsity Theatre** *(4375 W. 10th Ave.,* ☎ *290-0500)*, a charming little neighbourhood theatre (west), shows fine second-run films. Frequented mostly by people who live in the area.

Fifth Avenue Cinemas *(2110 Burrard St.,* ☎ *734-7469)* present excellent, very recent repertory films, including many in French with English subtitles. A good spot.

Calendar of Events

January

The **Polar Bear Swim** takes place every year on the morning of January 1st. Hundreds of people actually choose to take a swim lasting a few minutes in the freezing waters of English Bay. This event is always covered by the media. If you don't feel brave enough to challenge that icy water yourself, you can always go there and watch or see it on T.V.

Chinese New Year *(*☎ *687-6021)*. *Gung Hai Fat Choy!* means "Happy New Year!" in Chinese. The date is determined by the lunar calendar, therefore it varies every year, but celebrations are usually held around the end of January or the beginning of February. Traditional Dragon parades are organized in Chinatown and in Richmond.

The **Women in View** festival *(*☎ *685-6684)* highlights the work of female performers. Theatre, dance, comedy and music are all represented. A great festival.

The **Pacific International Auto & Light Truck Show** *(BC Place Stadium,* ☎ *294-8330)* is the only car show in British Columbia. Over 300 vehicles of all makes. If you want to see the brand-new American models up close, this is a good opportunity.

February

The **Spring Home Show** is the biggest home show in Western Canada, which takes place under the BC Place stadium dome.

South of the Border, Candlelight & Wine *(Vancouver Hotel,* ☎ *738-6822)*. Every year, music and dancing liven up this joyous evening.

March

The **BC Great Outdoors Show** is the place to be for camping and hunting enthusiasts, as well as for anglers.

Vancouver Storytelling Festival. For three days in March, storytellers gather in the West End are and practice their art in front of a captivated audience.

April

The **Vancouver Playhouse International Wine Festival** is an important festival where bottles of wine are auctioned and hundreds of wine growers gather to discuss their art and offer samples.

The Vancouver Sun Fun Run. During the third week of April, over 10,000 people participate in this celebration of sports and spring.

May

Cloverdale Rodeo. If you're in Vancouver and have never been to a rodeo, this is definitely the occasion. It's considered one of the most important in North America.

The **Vancouver International Children's Festival** *(☎ 687-7697)* is one of the biggest children's events in British Columbia with comedy, singing and dance performances.

The **Vancouver International Marathon** starts at the Plaza of Nations, then goes through Stanley Park to North Vancouver,

ENTERTAINMENT

and back to Vancouver. Over 4,000 runners take part in this major sporting event on the first Sunday of May.

The **Vancouver International Children's Festival** *(Vanier Park, ☎ 687-7697)* takes place the last week of May under characteristically red and white tents. Children come from all over British Columbia for this big festival in the beautiful setting of Vanier Park, where 70,000 people gather every year.

June

Spike & Mike's Animation Festival *(Ridge Cinema, 3131 Arbutus St., ☎ 738-6311)* presents the best animation from all over the world every year from the end of May to the end of June.

International Dragon Boat Festival *(False Creek, ☎ 687-2387)*. Long dug-out boats in the Chinese tradition, from all over the world, compete in these friendly races on the calm waters of False Creek.

Vancouver International Jazz Festival *(☎ 682-0706)*. Fans can come and satisfy their hunger for jazz at this distinguished festival. Artists perform throughout the city and the surrounding area.

Bard on the Beach *(Vanier Park, ☎ 737-0625 or 739-0559)* is an annual event in honour of Shakespeare. Plays are presented under a large tent, on the peninsula facing English Bay.

July

The **Benson & Hedges Symphony of Fire** *(English Bay, ☎ 738-4304)* is an international fireworks festival. A barge on English Bay, which serves as the base of operations, is the centre of attention. Dazzling show, guaranteed thrills.

Vancouver Chamber Music Festival *(☎ 736-6034)*. In the last week of July and the first week of August, six concerts are presented featuring young soloists.

Vancouver Early Music Festival *(☎ 732-1610)*. The music department of the University of British Columbia (UBC) hosts a series of baroque and medieval concerts played with period instruments.

August

The **Vancouver Folk Music Festival** *(☎ 602-9798)* has become a tradition in Vancouver. It takes place during the third week of August and features musicians from all over the world, from sunrise to sunset on Jericho Beach.

Abbotsford International Airshow *(Abbotsford, ☎ 852-9011)*. Here in Abbotsford, approximately 100 kilometres east of Vancouver, both young and old will be dazzled by F-16's, F-117 Stealths, and Migs. There are also are also old airplanes and clothing accessories. Don't forget your aviator glasses and sunscreen.

Vancouver International Comedy Festival *(☎ 683-0883)*. Every year on Granville Island comics provide several days of laughs.

The **Vancouver Fringe Festival** *(☎ 873-3646)* presents 10 days of theatre including original pieces by contemporary writers.

At the **Greater Vancouver Open** *(Northview Golf and Country, Surry, ☎ 899-4641)*, the biggest names in golf compete on a splendid course.

September

Molson Indy Vancouver *(BC Place Stadium, False Creek, ☎ 684-4639, tickets ☎ 280-INDY)*. In the heart of downtown, a course is set up where Indy racing cars (the North American equivalent of formula 1) compete in front of 100,000 enthusiastic spectators.

The **Terry Fox Run** *(from Ceperley Park to Stanley Park, ☎ 464-2666)*, on foot, bicycle or roller-blades, from one to 10 kilometres in length, is a fundraising event for cancer research. The run is in memory of the young athlete, Terry Fox, who initiated it.

ENTERTAINMENT

October

Vancouver International Film Festival *(☎ 685-0260)*. Vancouver, "Hollywood North", plays host to this increasingly significant festival which offers film buffs up to 150 films from all over the world.

Vancouver Writers and Readers Festival *(☎ 681-6330)*. During the third week of October, for five days, at least 50 writers from Canada and abroad meet with the public. Conferences and readings.

November

The **Annual Antique Show** *(Vancouver Trade & Convention Centre, ☎ 1-800-667-0619)* is an up-and-coming event featuring furniture and *objects d'art* from the 18th and 19th centuries, as well as from the beginning of the 20th.

December

The **Christmas Carol Ship Parade** *(English Bay Harbour, Burrard Inlet, ☎ 878-9988)*, an unusual and heartwarming procession of boats covered with lights, adds to the Christmas spirit. A family event.

The **VanDusen Garden's Festival of Lights** *(☎ 878-9274)* is another festival for the whole family. Throughout the Christmas season the VanDusen botanical garden is decorated with lights.

 SPECTATOR SPORTS

Hockey

Vancouver Canucks *(General Motors Place, ☎ 899-GOAL)*. The most popular sport in Canada, hockey lives up to its name in Vancouver. Fans here take the sport very seriously and attend games in droves. GM Place Stadium boasts a brand new ice rink. Getting there is very simple thanks to the Skytrain and the stadium's downtown location.

Baseball

Vancouver Canadians *(Nat Bailey Stadium,* ☎ *872-5232)*. Vancouverites may not consider baseball their favourite sport, but the city boasts a professional team nonetheless. Games take place during the summer.

Basketball

Vancouver Grizzlies *(General Motors Place,* ☎ *899-HOOP)*. Though Vancouver's brand-new professional basketball team does not always come out on top, it does provide a first-class show. Pro basketball games are somewhat rare in Canada. The newly built stadium is downtown and therefore easy to reach via the Skytrain.

Football

The **B.C. Lions** *(B.C. Place Stadium,* ☎ *280-4400)* have been spared the sort of financial trouble that has plagued many other Canadian Football League teams. Games against the Toronto Argonauts or the Montreal Alouettes are especially exciting.

Soccer

Vancouver Eighty-Sixers *(Swangard Stadium, Boundary, Kingsway to Imperial, Burnaby,* ☎ *299-0086)*. Though many young people — including a large number of girls — practise soccer here, professional teams do not draw the general public. Only European immigrants attend the games at Swangard Stadium to encourage players who, for that matter, are also mainly of European origin.

ENTERTAINMENT

Roller Hockey

Vancouver Voodoo *(Pacific Coliseum, ☎ 253-3336)*. Inspired by street hockey, roller hockey is a very popular sport among young boys in Vancouver. Small wonder then, that a semi-professional team was formed.

SHOPPING

Y ou'll surely come upon all manner of interesting shops as you explore the city. To help you discover some of the best bets in Vancouver however, read on...

MALLS, DEPARTMENT STORES AND MARKETS

Downtown

The **Pacific Centre** *(from Robson St. to Dunsmuir St., ☎ 688-7236)* is the largest shopping centre in the city. Approximately 300 quality boutiques offer a complete range of everything from jewellery and clothes to top-of-the-line items. Clothing and accessories at the Hermès and Louis Vuitton boutiques in Holt Renfrew; a fitness equipment store; a Ticketmaster; The Bay and Eaton's as well as Le Château, which mainly caters to a young clientele, are all to be found here. Parking fee.

Pacific Centre Mall *(underground at the corner of Howe St. and Georgia Ave.)* is a big shopping centre located right downtown. The latest in fashion from Paris to Tokyo, including of course the West Coast is available here. There are close to 200 shops.

The Bay *(at Granville and Georgia)*. Right downtown, this large, luxurious department store offers over six floors of designer and brand-name clothing and accessories, a huge perfume department with Chanel, Lancôme, Saint-Laurent, Clinique and more, as well as counters displaying precious jewellery and objects, all at very competitive prices. There are restaurants and a bar on various floors, and a catering service with coffee tables in the basement. They offer many promotions on Saturdays and Sundays.

Eaton's *(at Granville and Robson)* has the same formula as The Bay, selling clothing and everything for the home, with big fashion names in all departments. Competitive prices; restaurants; numerous promotions, especially on Saturday mornings.

Waterfront Centre *(at the base of the Waterfront Hotel, Canada Place)*: souvenir shops, flowers and cigars; tourist information counter; insurance company; hair salon; shoe repairs; a Starbucks coffeeshop; and a handful of small fast-food counters featuring various national cuisines.

West End

Robson Market *(Robson St. at Cardero)*. Vegetables; fresh fish, some of it cleaned and scaled; stands with fruit salads; meats, sausages and ham; pastries and other baked goods; a counter for Alsatian and German specialties; flowers and plants; vitamins and natural products; natural medicine clinic; hair salon; small restaurants upstairs. The market is covered, but well lit.

Burrard Inlet

Lonsdale Quay Market *(123 Carries Cates Court, North Vancouver, right near the Seabus terminal)*. A charming market, beautiful shops, a multitude of fast-food counters – all of it made a little more lively by artists performing on the seaside terrace.

False Creek

Granville Island Market *(9am to 6pm; Granville Island)* is Vancouver's best-known and most popular market. An immense commercial area surrounded by water with a fairground atmosphere. Good food, some of it prepared; fresh, good-quality vegetables, some of it organic; fresh fish and meat; wholesome breads; fast-food counters; pleasant shops selling jewellery, clothing and equipment for water sports and outdoor activities. Take a day to look, sample and wander. Parking is hard to find on the street but there are two indoor, pay parking lots nearby.

South Vancouver and Shaughnessy

Oakridge Centre *(Cambie St. and 41st Ave., ☎ 261-2511)*. Clothing boutiques, some of which feature French or British designers such as Rodier Paris; optical wear boutique; restaurants; The Bay; Zellers. Free parking.

The **Park Royal Shopping Centre** *(Marine Dr., West Vancouver, 5 min from Lions Gate, ☎ 925-9576)* is the most comprehensive shopping centre in West Vancouver comprising over 250 boutiques, banks, Coast Mountain and Cypress Mountain sports clothing stores as well as a Future Shop, which carries all brand-name electronics at the most competitive prices. Free parking.

 ACCESSORIES

I Love Hats *(1509 W. Broadway, at Granville St., ☎ 739-0200)*. All sorts of hats in all colours: traditional, modern or fun. Original sunglasses too.

 ART SUPPLIES

Maxwell's Artists' Materials *(206 Cambie St. at Water St.)*. As its name indicates, this shop specializes in artists' materials.

SHOPPING

BOOKSTORES

Duthie's *(919 Robson St., ☎ 684-4496)* is *the* bookstore in Vancouver. With an exceptional selection of books and a friendly attentive staff, Duthie's has built itself quite a reputation. They recently opened a branch *(☎ 602-0610)* in the impressive new Vancouver Library (see p 82). The move has been a huge success leaving people wondering why no one thought of doing it before!

Douglas Coupland

Vancouver can be proud of its most recent star-author, Douglas Coupland, who in 1991 at the age of 30 published his first novel, *Generation X*. His work coined a new catch-phrase that is now used by everyone from sociologists to ad agencies to describe this young, educated and underemployed generation. Coupland's latest novel *Microserfs*, has proven just as sociological, but this time it is the world of young computer whizzes that he describes, with sweeping generalizations about American popular culture that are both ironic and admiring; interestingly parallelling English-Canadian sentiment about the United States. Coupland works one day a week at Duthie's Bookstore *(4th Ave.)*.

Little Sisters Book and Art Emporium *(every day 10am to 11pm; 1238 Davie St., ☎ 669-1753 or 1-800-567-1662)*. This is the only gay bookshop in Western Canada. It offers gay literature as well as essays on homosexuality, feminism, etc. It is also a vast bazaar, with products that include humorous greeting cards. With the support of several Canadian literary figures, this bookshop has been fighting Canada Customs, which arbitrarily blocks the importation of certain publications. Books by recognized and respected authors such as Marcel Proust have been seized by Canada Customs, which has taken on the role of censor. Some of the same titles bound for regular bookshops have mysteriously escaped seizure by Canada Customs, leading to questions about discrimination.

Little Sisters

Little Sisters Book and Art Emporium has been engaged in a long battle with Canada Customs over the importation of books that Canada Customs deems offensive. The store became a target of Canada Customs, who repeatedly opened, inspected and occasionally confiscated Little Sisters' shipments. Little Sisters took Canada Customs to B.C. Supreme Court, which ruled that Canada Customs had a right to inspect, but that the agency's conduct infringed upon gays' and lesbians' freedom of speech rights and ultimately their equality. Little Sisters continues to fight Canada Customs' methods of detention, seizure, destruction and banning of books and magazines.

Manhattan Books *(1089 Robson St., ☎ 681-9074)* sells major international magazine and newspapers as well as a respectable selection of books in French.

Oscar's Art Books & Books *(1533 W. Broadway, at Granville, ☎ 731-0533)*. A large selection of fiction and books on art, cooking, nature, anatomy, travel... Wonderful books at low prices.

UBC Bookstore *(6200 University Blvd., ☎ 822-BOOK)* is the largest bookstore west of the Rockies with more than 100,000 titles. Allow enough time to park your car as the parking situation at UBC can be a problem.

 # CLOTHING

Below the Belt *(1131 Robson St., ☎ 688-6878)*, though a bit pricey, is a favourite with fashionable teens, but also with those for whom the *look* is paramount.

Dorothy Grant *(757 W. Hastings St., ☎ 681-0201)* makes clothing styled after that of the Haida Indians. The coats and capes are especially outstanding.

SHOPPING

Nicole Adrienne *(2705 Granville St., ☎ 738-8187)*. A colourful selection of women's clothing, in styles that are modern yet classic. Affordable prices.

Laura Ashley *(1171 Robson St., ☎ 688-8729)* is an English-style women's boutique with flowered dresses and embroidered knits in pastel colours. Affordable prices.

Second Suit *(2036 W. 4th Ave., ☎ 732-0338)* carries the best in formal men's wear from Armani to Boss and Dior.

Tilley Endurables *(2401 Granville St., ☎ 732-4287)*. Fine-quality clothing in elegant styles for casual wear, but also for hikers and adventurers. Pants, shorts, shirts, safari jackets, windbreakers and raincoats, all made of cotton, in grey, blue, white and beige.

True Value Vintage *(710 Robson St., ☎ 685-5403)* is an exceptional shop that both buys and sells vintage clothing from the glory days of rockabilly and disco.

 ## ELECTRONICS

A&B Sound *(556 Seymour St., ☎ 687-5837)* has great prices in electronics, video cassettes and compact discs. Watch out for the crowds on weekends.

 ## FOOD

Capers *(1675 Robson St., ☎ 687-5288)*, is a natural food store that carries fresh vegetables, meats, prepared dishes, good breads and vitamins. Somewhat expensive but practical for travellers. You can eat here.

Chocolat Daniel *(1105 Robson St., ☎ 688-9624)*. One of the rare fine-chocolate shops in Vancouver, and probably the best. The dark chocolate and truffles, prepared in strict Belgian tradition, are exceptional. Small figurines, boxes and vases enhance their presentation and make lovely gifts. The prices are reasonable. There are seven more Chocolat Daniels throughout the city; call the number listed above for their locations.

Kobayashi Shoten *(1518 Robson St., ☎ 683-1019)* is a Japanese store that sells groceries, take-out meals and gifts as well as table settings and linens.

Meinhart *(3002 Granville St., ☎ 732-4405)*. Another health-food store. Same formula as Capers but smaller, with more of a family atmosphere. They sell Godiva chocolates and lovely fresh flowers. A bit expensive.

Old Vienna Bakery *(2546 Granville St., ☎ 730-0304)*. Viennese bakery-pastry shop. Traditional bread and cakes; sandwiches, soups and coffee at affordable prices.

Rocky Mountain Chocolate Factory *(1017 Robson St., ☎ 688-4100)* is a divine little chocolate shop. You can savour bulk chocolate with nuts and fruits, or perhaps the bitter dark chocolate, for the real connoisseur.

The **Ten Ren Tea and Ginseng Company** *(550 Main St., ☎ 684-1566)* is without a doubt the best tea shop in Canada. Big jars hold an exceptional variety of teas from around the world.

 ## GIFTS

Alders Duty-Free *(1026 Alberni St.)*. Internationally renowned, brand-name cosmetics, jewellery, leather goods, liquor and tobacco – all tax-free for tourists from outside Canada.

Atelier Nicole Dahan *(1529 W. 6th Ave., at the end of the Granville Bridge, ☎ 739-5725)*. Five minutes from Granville Island. Beautiful paintings of British Columbian landscapes and wildlife by this artist from Marseilles.

Crystal Gallery *(Lonsdale Quay Market, North Vancouver, ☎ 986-8224)*. Reasonably priced, attractive, brightly coloured crystal objects.

Edinburgh Tartan Shop *(901 W. Pender St., at Hornby, ☎ 688-8755)*. A Scottish boutique with jewellery and ready-made clothing from both Scotland and Wales. Very good quality and prices.

SHOPPING

Jade World *(1696 W. 1st Ave., ☎ 733-7212)*. Right near Granville Island. Jade sculptures and jewellery

Rasta Wares *(1505 Commercial Dr., ☎ 255-3600)*. This shop offers incense and jewellery from India, Indonesia and Africa at low prices.

Wendy's Collection *(2620 W. Broadway, ☎ 730-8387)*. The window catches your eye from a distance. The shop sells superb statuettes and sculptures from China. Jewellery and gemstones at affordable prices.

 HAIRDRESSERS

Suki's Hair Salon *(3157 S. Granville St., at 16th Ave., ☎ 738-7713)*. Vancouver's most fashionable hair salon, frequented by the jetset. They offer a wide range of services at affordable prices.

 HOME DECOR

Hana Gallery *(2435 Granville St., ☎ 736-8473)*. One of the rare stores selling Japanese antiques. Beautiful furniture and accessories imported from Japan.

Kim-John *(2903 Granville St., at 13th Ave., ☎ 925-9966)*. Articles for your house and dining-room table in fine Chinese or British porcelain (Wedgewood, Royal Doulton), Bohemian crystal or solid silver at 50% off regular prices. A multitude of attractive, affordably priced objects.

The Kitchen Corner *(2686 Granville St., ☎ 739-4422)*. You'll find absolutely everything in this little store for next to nothing: anything you might need for your kitchen, for camping, a day at the beach as well as spices, candles, souvenirs...

MUSIC

Highlife Records & Music *(1317 Commercial Dr.,* ☎ *251-6964)*. This is the spot to find new wave and other types of music at good prices.

HMV *(1160 Robson St.)* is the mega-store for music, with great prices on new releases. The store is open late on weekends.

 # NATIVE ARTS AND CRAFTS

The **Inuit Gallery of Vancouver** *(345 Water St.,* ☎ *688-7323)* sells some magnificent pieces of native art from Canada's far north and from the Queen Charlotte Islands.

Khot-La-Cha *(270 Whonoak St., North Vancouver)*. One block from Marine Drive and McGuire Street. Beautiful native sculptures from the Salish Coast.

Leona Lattimer *(1590 W. 2nd Ave., west of Granville Island,* ☎ *732-4556)* is a lovely gallery where you can admire some fine native art or if you like, purchase a piece. Quality jewellery and prints. Expensive.

The Raven and The Bear *(1528 Duranleau St., Granville Island,* ☎ *669-3990)*. Excellent-quality native works at reasonable prices. Lithographs, sculptures and natural stonework.

The **Silver Gallery** *(126 Robson St.,* ☎ *681-6884)* is the least expensive store for fine-quality jewellery and native crafts. Solid silver bracelets, necklaces and rings with gold enamelling, at competitive prices. They also sell Indonesian objects, including masks, at affordable prices.

Spirit Wrestler Gallery *(8 Water St.,* ☎ *669-8813)*. Attractive sculptures and paintings by Inuit artists and artists from the northwest coast.

SHOPPING

NEWSPAPERS

Mayfair News *(1535 W. Broadway, ☎ 738-8951)*. Newspapers and magazines from all over the world in every language, sometimes a bit later than the original issue date.

OPTOMETRISTS

Lenscrafters *(Pacific Centre, ☎ 685-1024)*. One-hour service, efficient and reliable; wide selection of fashionable frames.

Regency Contact Lens *(607-650 W. 41st Ave., Oakridge Center, entrance on Cambie St., ☎ 263-0900)*. Contact lens specialists, offering quality service and competitive prices.

PHARMACIES

Gaia Garden Herbal Apothecary *(2672 W. Broadway, ☎ 734-4372)*. The only place in town that has everything in the way of herbal medicines. Visa cards accepted.

Shoppers Drug Mart *(many locations throughout the city; the following two are open 24 hours a day: 1125 Davie St., ☎ 669-2424, 2302 W. 4th Ave., ☎ 738-3138)* has a bit of everything: pharmacist, cosmetics, items for the home, pop, juice, a few groceries.

Tung Fong Hung *(536 Main St., ☎ 688-0883)* is a traditional Chinese herbalist. Ask for Liping, he will take the time to explain the complex healing powers of these plants. The shop specializes in ginseng.

SHOES

David Gordon *(1202 Robson St., ☎ 685-3784)* is a typical western shoe store with boots, shoes and sandals. It's been in business since 1976 and has a good reputation.

Stéphane de Raucourt Shoes *(1067 Robson St., ☎ 681-8814)*. If you are looking for quality shoes that stand out from the ordinary, here is a spot to keep in mind. They are expensive, but a little window-shopping never hurt anyone.

 SOUVENIRS

Made in Canada Shopping *(1060 Robson St., ☎ 682-2627)*. A large selection of souvenirs, clothing and silver jewellery.

Robson Souvenirs Centre *(1222 Robson St., ☎ 683-9686)* offers a wide selection of Canadian, North American and native souvenirs. They also sell smoked and canned salmon, as well as maps and travel guides of the area.

 SPORTS

Altus Mountain Gear *(137 W. Broadway, ☎ 876-5255)*. Everything for mountaineering: waterproof gear, clothing, tents, backpacks and more at cost price or for rent.

A stop at **Coast Mountain Sports** *(2201 W. 4th Ave., ☎ 731-6181)* is a must for mountaineers who appreciate quality equipment. Only the best is sold here, and the shop is therefore quite expensive and reserved mostly for pros. The staff is very friendly and experienced.

Cyclepath *(1421 W. Broadway, one block east of Granville St.)*. This bike shop does repairs and sells all sorts of bicycles and accessories.

Ecomarine Granville Island *(1668 Durenleau St., ☎ 689-7575)* has everything for fans of sea-kayaking. You can even try out the kayaks before you buy.

Mountain Equipment Co-op *(130 W. Broadway, ☎ 872-7858)*. This giant store offers everything you need for your outdoor activities. You must be a member to make purchases; but membership only costs five dollars.

Ruddick's Fly Fishing *(1654 Duranleau St., Granville Island,* ☎ *681-3747)* is a wonderful store for fly-fishing fans that even inspires newcomers to the sport. There are thousands of different flies for all sorts of fish. The owner will be glad to assist you. They also sell super-light canes, state-of-the-art fishing reels, souvenir clothing as well as fishing-related sculptures and gadgets.

Seymour Bicycle Fitness *(1775 W. 4th Ave., just east of Burrard St.,* ☎ *737-9889)*. Bikes, clothing, accessories and parts. All the well-known brands. This store differentiates itself from others by specializing in bicycles and accessories for women.

Taiga Works *(390 W. 8th Ave.)* is a small shop with mountain sports equipment and prices that beat the competition. Gore-Tex is at half-price. A good address to remember.

3 Vets *(2200 Yukon St.,* ☎ *872-5475)* is a local institution. For 40 years this store has been supplying reasonably priced camping equipment to everyone from professional lumberjacks to tree planters and weekend campers.

 STATIONARY

Kinko's Copies *(24 hours a day; 1900 W. Broadway,* ☎ *734-2697)*. Computers and photocopy machines, as well as paper and office supplies. Everything you would need, at low prices, to create CV's, files and documents yourself, with the help of their knowledgeable staff.

INDEX

INDEX

INDEX

■ ULYSSES TRAVEL GUIDES

□ Affordable B&Bs
  in Québec . . . . . $12.95 CAN
                        $9.95 US

□ Atlantic Canada $24.95 CAN
                        $17.95 US

□ Beaches of Maine $12.95 CAN
                        $9.95 US

□ Bahamas . . . . . $24.95 CAN
                        $17.95 US

□ Calgary . . . . . . $17.95 CAN
                        $12.95 US

□ Canada . . . . . . $29.95 CAN
                        $21.95 US

□ Chicago . . . . . . $19.95 CAN
                        $14.95 US

□ Chile . . . . $27.95 CAN
                        $17.95 US

□ Costa Rica . . . . $27.95 CAN
                        $19.95 US

□ Cuba . . . . $24.95 CAN
                        $17.95 US

□ Dominican
  Republic . . . . . . $24.95 CAN
                        $17.95 US

□ Ecuador Galapagos
  Islands . . . . $24.95 CAN
                        $17.95 US

□ El Salvador . . . . $22.95 CAN
                        $14.95 US

□ Guadeloupe . . . $24.95 CAN
                        $17.95 US

□ Guatemala . . . . $24.95 CAN
                        $17.95 US

□ Honduras . . . . . $24.95 CAN
                        $17.95 US

□ Jamaica . . . . . . $24.95 CAN
                        $17.95 US

□ Lisbon . . . . $18.95 CAN
                        $13.95 US

□ Louisiana . . . . . $29.95 CAN
                        $21.95 US

□ Martinique . . . . $24.95 CAN
                        $17.95 US

□ Montréal . . . . . $19.95 CAN
                        $14.95 US

□ New Orleans . . $17.95 CAN
                        $12.95 US

□ New York City . $19.95 CAN
                        $14.95 US

□ Nicaragua . . . . $24.95 CAN
                        $16.95 US

□ Ontario . . . . . . $24.95 CAN
                        $14.95US

□ Ottawa . . . . . . $17.95 CAN
                        $12.95 US

□ Panamá . . . . . . $24.95 CAN
                        $16.95 US

□ Portugal . . . . . . $24.95 CAN
                        $16.95 US

□ Provence - Côte
  d'Azur . . . . $29.95 CAN
                        $21.95US

□ Québec . . . . . . $29.95 CAN
                        $21.95 US

□ Québec and Ontario
  with Via . . . . $9.95 CAN
                        $7.95 US

□ Toronto . . . . . . $18.95 CAN
                        $13.95 US

□ Vancouver . . . . $17.95 CAN
                        $12.95 US

□ Washington D.C. $18.95 CAN
                        $13.95 US

□ Western Canada $29.95 CAN
                        $21.95 US

■ ULYSSES DUE SOUTH

□ Acapulco . . . . . $14.95 CAN
                        $9.95 US

□ Belize . . . . $16.95 CAN
                        $12.95 US

□ Cartagena
  (Colombia) . . . . $12.95 CAN
                        $9.95 US

□ Cancun Cozumel $17.95 CAN
                        $12.95 US

□ Puerto Vallarta . $14.95 CAN
                        $9.95 US

□ St. Martin and
  St. Barts . . . . . $16.95 CAN
                        $12.95 US

■ ULYSSES GREEN ESCAPES

☐ Cycling in France $22.95 CAN
$16.95 US
☐ Hiking in the Northeastern
United States . . $19.95 CAN
$13.95 US
☐ Hiking in Québec $19.95 CAN
$13.95 US

■ ULYSSES TRAVEL JOURNAL

☐ Ulysses Travel Journal
(Blue, Red, Green,
Yellow, Sextant) . $9.95 CAN
$7.95 US

QUANTITY	TITLES	PRICE	TOTAL

NAME:_____	Sub-total
ADDRESS:_____	Postage & Handling $8.00*
_____	Sub-total
Payment: ☐ Money Order ☐ Visa ☐	G.S.T.in Canada 7%
Card	TOTAL
Signature:_____	

ULYSSES TRAVEL PUBLICATIONS
4176 St-Denis, Montréal, QC, H2W
2M5
(514) 843-9447 fax (514) 843-
9448
www.ulysse.ca
* $15 for overseas orders

U.S. ORDERS: **GLOBE PEQUOT
PRESS**
P.O. Box 833, 6 Business Park Road,
Old Saybrook, CT 06475-0833
1-800-243-0495 fax 1-800-820-
2329
www.globe-pequot.com

80025 75540